> **"No matter what your path looks like,
> I believe it starts with relationships.
> Building them, maintaining them,
> and valuing them for the long term."**

Plenty of businesses exist, but only some get lifelong customers. So how do you create something genuine that's built to last?

Emily Frisella, a multi-passionate entrepreneur, knows that authentic connections are the answer a lot of businesses are missing. In *Relationships First*, she shares lessons from her business and coaching to guide you toward the work ethic, communication skills, and personal values every business needs to succeed.

With her "no woo-woo" approach, Emily shows why genuine relationships are the secret ingredient to success in every area of business and life.

Inside this book, Emily shares practical advice on how to use her key tenets, including:

- respect the potential and significance of every person
- show appreciation and gratitude
- demonstrate personal accountability
- make it your best work and create a culture of improvement
- have fun, act with integrity, and think big

This business leadership book combines personal development with strategic relations principles.

Level up your business and learn why a relationships-first mentality is a mindset for success.

1

RELATIONSHIPS FIRST
PEOPLE
PASSION
& PROFIT

EMILY
FRISELLA

Relationships First © copyright 2022 by Emily Frisella.
All rights reserved. No part of this book may be reproduced in any form
whatsoever, by photography or xerography or by any other means,
by broadcast or transmission, by translation into any kind of language,
nor by recording electronically or otherwise, without permission
in writing from the author, except by a reviewer, who may
quote brief passages in critical articles or reviews.

ISBN 13: 978-1-63489-569-9

Library of Congress Catalog Number has been applied for.
Printed in the United States of America
First Printing: 2022
26 25 24 23 22   5 4 3 2 1

Design by Cindy Samargia Laun

Wise Ink Creative Publishing
807 Broadway St. NE, Suite 46
Minneapolis, MN 55413
wiseink.com

RELATIONSHIPS FIRST

PEOPLE PASSION & PROFIT

EMILY FRISELLA

FOREWORD

I received a text from Emily asking what I was doing, so I immediately responded, "Why? Are you here?" and started walking toward the front door to greet her. It turns out she wasn't there—in fact, she was getting ready to place the phone call that led to me writing this foreword.

But if you want to know the type of person Emily is, that text conversation will explain it. It is not unlike her to take a flight and show up at my front doorstep if she feels like I need her. You're probably asking yourself, *Who are you?* I am a nobody. That's precisely what I said when Emily asked me to write this foreword. But to Emily, it doesn't matter who you are; she will make you feel like somebody.

As soon as we hung up the phone, I thought, "How the hell do you write a foreword?" Typically, if someone asked me to do this, I would immediately call Emily and ask her what to include. But, given that she trusted me enough to ask me to write it, I didn't want to make her nervous by asking how—instead, I turned to my next-best reliable source of information, Google. The first thing I came across said, "Stay honest. Flattery has no room in the foreword." I laughed out loud.

Here is the thing: if you are honest about Emily, it is flattery. I once told her that I felt like I had been lied to. All my life, I have heard perfection doesn't exist, and then I met her. (She will try to have this part removed. Dear editors, please keep it in the book.)

Emily is just as kind as she is beautiful. She is just as successful as she is humble. She is the most caring person you will ever meet. She remembers everything: dog names, friends of friends' names, your birthday, the day you got married, and even the silly little desires (like a $300 coconut cake) that you once mentioned in passing. She responds to your messages and calls like you are the only person in the world trying to get in touch with her, when in actuality, it is quite the opposite.

When my mom was diagnosed with pancreatic cancer, I only had a few minutes to talk to someone, and Emily was the first call I made. I could hear the busyness of her day in the background, but she stopped everything and cried with me for the brief few seconds I had to get it off my chest, pick myself back up, and become a beacon of strength for my family. That is just who she is—she can be whatever you need her to be, and she does it so well.

In addition to my personal relationship with Emily, she is also the first person I call when I need business advice. I remember when I was working my first retail deal, I had no clue what I was doing. The buyer would send me an email, and it was like Greek to me! I wanted to respond immediately so they thought I was seasoned at this. Still, it was quite literally the opposite, so I would frantically call Emily and ask her what I needed to say. She would send rapid-fire answers as if she had already been briefed on how the questions were going to go. I guess being an entrepreneur for twenty years is its own kind of briefing, but when the dust settled, I was astounded by the wealth of knowledge she holds in that tiny little head of hers.

(Actually, if you have ever met Emily in person, she is not tiny. She is strikingly gorgeous, tall, and captivating. Wait, no flattery. Got it. Honest? Yes.)

I ended up flying to Saint Louis, and we went to the mall together to see my products in the store for the first time. She celebrated my victory as if it were her own, and it is still my fondest business memory to date. If there will ever be one to replace it, she will without a doubt be there. And if you are still thinking about "that one phone call," I am sure she would be my first phone call if I ever got arrested.

Emily is a wealth of knowledge. There is no problem too big for her to solve. When I first arrived at the concept of my business, I knew that I wanted Emily to be involved. I knew that I needed a mentor, and she was the one for me. If you are reading this book, you too will find many nuggets of information that will stick with you for a lifetime—golden nuggets, because anything Emily touches turns to gold. But she also makes sure that anything you touch will turn to gold. She wants success for you just as much as she wants success for herself. It's a cliché, I know, but she wears a crown while she straightens yours.

I have always said this since the day I met her—anyone in her life was always going to be good, but we are great because of her.

Emily, you are one of a kind, and one of my life's greatest gifts is knowing you.

googles "how to end a foreword"

Becky Peavy
Movéo Fit Co

CONTENTS

Introduction | 11

1 | Relationships First | 19

2 | Make It Your Best Work | 35

3 | Personal Accountability | 57

4 | Respect the Potential and Significance of Every Person | 75

5 | Never Compromise Truth | 91

6 | Act with Honesty and Integrity | 107

7 | Promote a Culture of Innovation and Continuous Improvement | 123

8 | Show Appreciation and Gratitude | 141

9 | Have Fun and Think Big | 155

Questions for Further Discussion | 169

About the Author | 184

*To Andy for understanding me, loving me,
and forever being my biggest supporter.*

*To my parents, who always believed in me
no matter what,
for showing me the value of a strong work ethic
and acting with integrity.*

INTRODUCTION

I WAS AN ENTREPRENEUR AT TWENTY YEARS OLD.

It all started the same way most entrepreneurs' stories start. I loved flowers, I loved making arrangements, and I loved events and parties. The three go hand in hand, right? So I took out a loan, bought a building and land, made some relationships with suppliers, and opened up my own business called Floral Boutique. If hashtags had been around during that time, mine might have included all the current trending ones that I personally can't stand: #girlboss #bosslife #blessed.

So there I was, a twenty-year-old from small-town Missouri with her own flower shop, plenty of business for her store, and six employees (*six!*), all of whom were older than me, who owed their livelihood to me. Me! #livingthedream (Another hashtag that makes me cringe.)

But the truth was that I had no idea what I was doing. I don't say that with false modesty—I actually mean it. I come from a family of entrepreneurs, so somewhere along the way I'd gotten it into my head that all the "stuff" that went along with owning my own business would just organically come to me.

Payroll? No problem! The money was coming in, the money would go out.

Seasonality? No big thing! My busy seasons would just magically make up for downtime.

Marketing? Not a concern. My store, my brand, would speak for itself.

(Writing this, I have to admit that I miss those carefree days of my early twenties . . .)

One day, an employee came to me holding her paycheck from the week before. "Emily," she said quietly. "I took this to the bank to cash it this morning, and they said there were insufficient funds."

My heart stopped. There must have been some sort of mistake. I was making tons of cash . . . wasn't I? This was before the days of online banking, so I took her check and proudly announced that I would be right back to "straighten all this out" with the bank. I think at that moment I actually believed that the bank had made a mistake.

You can imagine my horror when the bank teller told me the truth: I had $42.86 in my bank account. She went on to pull out the last few bank statements that I'd conveniently ignored. The numbers didn't lie. Each statement showed money coming in, a whole lot of money going out, and not a single mistake on their end.

No wonder my payroll check had bounced. Come to think of it, *I had a lot of other checks floating out there that were about to bounce too.*

What did I do, you ask?

Well, if you're thinking I put my ego aside, owned up to my mistakes, and lived happily ever after as a successful entrepreneur, you would be wrong.

Instead, I lied. I pulled cash from my personal savings, put it in my business account to cover my outstanding checks, and went back to my employees with a story about how "the bank messed up" and was going to straighten everything out.

Hey, I was twenty years old, okay? I've learned a lot since then.

Looking back, this moment of humiliation was one of the best things that could have happened to me. It forced me to admit there was a lot I didn't know about running a business. (Understatement of the year—maybe the century!) It forced me to be resourceful and resilient in the future. It boosted me to think of inventive ways to plan and create revenue. If it weren't for that moment in the bank, with $42.86 in my account and the sheer terror of knowing that I was in deep trouble, my mindset would have remained that all I needed was to "think positively" for my business to just naturally be a success.

I got past that particular setback and sold my flower shop after about four years in business. Since then, I have developed three other entrepreneurial ventures, which I'll talk about in this book. If you follow me on social media or have been part of my world in any way, you know that I've since figured out who I am, how I work best, and how to bounce back from difficulties as a business owner. Everyone loves a good comeback story, right? While it's true that a person could probably find me on Instagram and see the more glamorous side of entrepreneurship, I would be lying if I said I didn't think back to that pivotal moment in the bank often. And when I say often, I mean *all the time.*

And I think that's a good thing. When people ask me about my career journey, I don't want them to think that it's been all feel-good positivity. In fact, I cringe when I see people making money off the message that entrepreneurship begins and ends with "You can do it if you just believe in yourself!" I call that "woo-woo" mentality.

Don't get me wrong—it starts with passion. It starts with excitement and positive energy. But there's so much more. The truth is that there is a lot in the middle that can be messy and hard. There's a ton that you are going to have to face, own up to, and figure out on the road to becoming a successful entrepreneur, and *no one seems to be talking about those things.*

This book is not meant to sell you on the idea that you can't start your own business. You can! And let's just get this part out of the way first: I do believe in you, and you can do it!

Now that we've got the whole "empowerment" thing taken care of, can we move on to what really matters? Because those feel-good platitudes and fluffy messages aren't going to help you much when you find yourself in the bank looking at $42.86 to your name.

Trust me, I speak from experience.

The book you're reading is a compilation of the mistakes, messes, tips, and tricks that have seen me through to the other side of entrepreneurial success. No drama, no pretense, no BS.

Being an entrepreneur isn't all facts and figures. This is emotional work. I would never pretend otherwise. We're talking about passions here, not to mention people and relationships. That's exactly why I want to acknowledge and prepare you for the times you're frustrated, angry, overwhelmed, and maybe even sad. When you're doing something you love, business is personal. **What I want for you is to move past all that emotion to a place of action and ultimate success.**

As I considered how to organize my book, I kept falling back on the nine core values that have gotten me through the real ups and downs of entrepreneurship across all my businesses. I believe so strongly in these values that I literally have them hanging up on the wall in my offices. I want to see them all the time. I want to be reminded of them all the time. I want my employees to be reminded of them all the time. I mean, what's the point of having core values you only visit once or twice a year?

Don't mistake these for steps on a ladder—they aren't. You're going to have to navigate each one of these things on a daily basis, whether you like it or not. For me, these are non-negotiable values that every successful entrepreneur must embrace, even when it's hard. Even when it's messy.

What I want for you is to
MOVE PAST ALL THAT EMOTION
TO A **PLACE OF ACTION** AND **ULTIMATE SUCCESS.**

1
Have Fun and Think Big

2
Make It Your Best Work

3
Never Compromise Truth

4
Personal Accountability

5
Relationships-First Mentality

6
Act with Honesty and Integrity

7
Show Appreciation and Gratitude

8
Respect the Potential
and Significance of Every Person

9
Promote a Culture of Innovation
and Continuous Improvement

I've been inspired over the years by some really great people, all from different walks of life and experiences, and I've always learned best from the stories of others. I want you to use the tales in this book in the same way I have: as learning experiences and motivation. I want you to apply these lessons to your own journey, no matter what industry you are inspired to take part in.

Ultimately, I want this book to help you see the challenges you're bound to face as a business owner for what they are: gifts to help you reach your full potential. No avoiding your mistakes. No blaming your missteps on "the bank" or any other convenient scapegoat. You're a business owner now, and if you want to earn those glittery, Instagram-worthy vacation photos, you're going to have to work for them.

The work will sometimes be messy. But if you ask me, it's worth it.

THE WORK WILL SOMETIMES BE MESSY. BUT IF YOU ASK ME, IT'S WORTH IT.

1
RELATIONSHIPS FIRST

IT'S SAFE TO SAY THAT IF you had seen me in my formative years, you would not have guessed I'd be writing a book about being a female entrepreneur. Young Emily was chubby, shy, and never really felt like she fit in anywhere. All that would change when I joined FFA (Future Farmers of America) at age fourteen.

If you weren't raised in small-town Missouri like I was, you might not be familiar with FFA. Or maybe you've heard of it but think it's just a bunch of kids learning how to pick up after their farm animals and show steers at the local fairgrounds. Not so. To this day, I credit the Future Farmers of America for giving me confidence to speak up for myself, take on leadership roles, and become the risk-taker I would need to be in order to become a successful entrepreneur.

Don't get me wrong—my parents were amazing examples for me. My father was a lifelong entrepreneur, and I saw from him what the entrepreneurial life and rewards were like. I wanted that for myself, even at a young age. But wanting something and believing you can do it are two different things, especially when you're a shy small-town girl like I was.

The truth is that for me, middle school and junior high were a shit show. I had some mean teachers and dealt with some mean kids. I can see how a kid that age, going through all the turmoil that comes from growing up, is at risk of developing a mindset that will crush their dreams before they even get a chance to figure out what they are.

The FFA forced me to develop skills as a public speaker. Was it scary? Hell yes! But I did it. And every time I got up to speak in front of a crowd, I got better at it. I participated in knowledge competitions and ended up becoming president of my chapter. Eventually, I found my "voice." I remember thinking to myself, *You know what? I can do this.* **I have this in me.** It's a mindset that I've carried with me my entire life.

Here's the thing: every book on entrepreneurship in the world is going to tell you some version of this story, right? That all you have to do is believe in yourself, and the rest will just come to you because you deserve it? But here's what they leave out:

That mindset didn't put me on an easy path to success. Hardly. Once I figured out what I wanted, I knew I was going to have to work my ass off for it. And that's exactly what I did. By the time I was in eighth grade,

I was working at my local golf course, saving every single penny I could. I worked all through high school as a waitress and grocery store clerk. While my friends were partying and sleeping in on the weekends, I purposely asked for the busiest shifts on Friday, Saturday, and Sunday, when I knew I'd make the most tips.

I suppose you could say I "gave up" a lot during that time, but I didn't see it that way. I still don't. It was an investment in my future. My parents were incredibly supportive of me, and I'll always be grateful to them for that, but they never promised they would take care of me for all eternity. This was maybe their greatest gift to me of all.

If I wanted what my mom and dad had, I *knew* I was going to have to work for it. I had to create the discipline *within myself* that would take me where I wanted to go.

So will you.

WHO YOU KNOW

When you begin with this sort of work ethic at an early age and see the rewards start coming in, it's a huge advantage. It certainly was for me. But if you're reading this book well past your twenties and bartending days, don't sweat it. If you don't have a supportive family and can't see yourself waiting tables on holidays and weekends to make your dreams come true, that's fine too. You're going to see throughout this book that I'm all about giving you the chance to figure out the path that is best for *you*.

No matter what that path looks like, I believe it starts with relationships. Building them, maintaining them, and valuing them for the long term.

Look, I read a lot of books about entrepreneurship that start with the "big idea." They say that the thing you need to do is stay laser focused on making what you want happen.

It's not that this is bad advice. I'm definitely laser focused when it comes to my businesses and my brands. (We'll talk about this much more later in the book.) But I don't think it starts there.

NO MATTER WHAT THAT PATH LOOKS LIKE, I believe it starts with **RELATIONSHIPS.** **BUILDING** THEM, **MAINTAINING** THEM, AND **VALUING** THEM *for the long term.*

You know that old saying, "It's not what you know, it's who you know"? Well, I figured that out quickly when I was a teenager.

All those jobs I had? All those connections I was making?

Those relationships ended up being the most important ones of my life when, at the age of twenty, I started my own business.

People remembered me.

People liked me.

People *believed* in me.

It wasn't that I'd done anything special—I really was just working hard and treating people I worked with the way I would have wanted to be treated. Turns out the Golden Rule is "golden" for a reason.

By the time I opened the doors to my flower shop, I already had a huge support network of people who wanted to see me succeed. This went beyond my friends and family, into my wider community. They patronized my business, were excited for my success, and were an active part of spreading the word. And as we all know, there's nothing more powerful than a word-of-mouth recommendation in business!

I don't care how much the world changes in terms of products, technology, and innovation. **If you can set yourself up as someone who values relationships above all else, you are ahead of the competition. Of all the things that we use in business—machines, technology, supplies—the only thing that appreciates is people!** *Relationships! Invest in them and they will invest in you!*

This is a mantra I hold above all others in each of my businesses. Relationships first. Before the product, before the notoriety, and definitely before the money.

Relationships first.

WHAT CAN I GIVE?

Times have changed a lot since my flower-shop days, along with the way we do business. I am often approached by new entrepreneurs looking for quick tips for success; when I tell them to start with building relationships, I tend to hear things like:

I'm already doing that! I go to meetups, I try to connect, but it's just so much harder than I thought it was going to be.

I keep trying to build relationships with people, but no one ever responds to my messages or calls. What am I doing wrong?

Or my personal favorite (cough cough—sarcasm):
I just don't have time to build relationships.

Look—if you don't have time to build relationships, you should stop before you even get started. Relationships take effort, and *it's a required effort* in entrepreneurship.

What you're doing "wrong" is refusing to acknowledge that relationships, at least the ones that are truly going to impact your business in a positive way, take time.

This is true in life too, isn't it? You're not going to create a deep, trusting relationship with a friend or a spouse in a day or two. It takes time and patience.

So, great. You need patience and time. That should do it, right?

Not so fast.

Before you start creating these all-important relationships, you need to keep something really clear:

People can spot disingenuous relationship building from a mile away.

What do I mean by disingenuous relationship building? How about this:

Several years ago, I was at an event speaking about business and health, and how the two go hand in hand for high performance. It was such a fun event for me—I love talking about this stuff! After my talk, I was at the side of the stage, preparing to exit the venue, when a woman approached me. I'll call her Brenda. She began gushing over me, flattering me to the point of making me a little uncomfortable. I could tell she was trying to butter me up.

After a while, I tuned out her words. I kept thinking to myself, *This woman definitely wants something from me.* Brenda was totally oblivious to my body language and how I was receiving her "compliments"; she just kept on going. *Yep,* I thought to myself, *she wants something all right.*

Sure enough, she ended her pitch with, "So if you could tell your friends about my product, that would be great and would really help me out!"

Okay, let's back this train up and break down what went wrong here:

1. She cornered me and poured on flattery. It felt fake and awkward. Not just "felt" that way—it *was* fake and awkward.
2. I had never met her before in my life, and we had no connections that she mentioned. She just talked at me as though I were supposed to reciprocate her energy.
3. I had never even heard of her product, let alone any information on what it did or why I should care about it.
4. She spent *zero* time or effort working to build a relationship with me. Giving someone a bunch of BS "You're so amazing!" compliments is *not* relationship building.
5. She had the audacity to ask me to promote her (in other words, leverage my supporters) to friends and customers I had worked *years* to build and establish trusting relationships with.
6. She made the entire purpose of our little "meeting" about her and what she needed.

I see this type of "relationship building" happening *all the time,* and it is so off-putting. Brenda achieved the exact opposite of what she wanted to with me. I knew after that interaction that I never wanted to do business with her and didn't care one bit about the product she was selling.

It's really simple when you think about it. You need to give, give, and give some more before you try to "cash in" anything in a business relationship. And even if you never make a sale or a dime off that person, that needs to be okay too. You have to lead with creating a real, honest relationship, not with greed.

Look, I get it. If you have a goal of owning your own business, it can be easy to just chase that almighty dollar. If you want to reach out to someone for their support, it's natural to be focused on what this person can do for you.

But guess what? The opposite mindset is going to be what creates a relationship.

Instead of focusing on what other people can do for you, figure out what you can do for them.

Brenda could have made that interaction I mentioned above a whole lot different had she embraced this mentality.

INSTEAD OF FOCUSING ON WHAT OTHER PEOPLE CAN DO FOR YOU, figure out **WHAT YOU CAN DO FOR THEM.**

If you're still stumped on how she blew it with me, let's break it down:
1. Instead of opening by pouring on flattery, she could have asked an interesting, thought-provoking question. Surface-level shit doesn't stick in someone's mind. Show the person that you respect them as an individual.
2. She could have mentioned a mutual thought we shared based upon the talk I just gave on stage and how that applied in her life. At that moment, I was still on a high from my talk—it would have been a perfect time to keep that momentum going.
3. She could have shared her passion behind her product and what inspired her to launch it. People's genuine enthusiasm for their business can be infectious.
4. She could have asked me what she could do to help me. I'm not saying this because I'm selfish or self-serving, but as a simple fact: asking what you can do for someone else shows genuine care and interest. Even a little of this goes a long way.

You guys, this isn't rocket science. It's don't-be-a-turd-and-try-to-use-people science.

Honestly, not taking relationship building seriously is one of the biggest mistakes I see people make. That's why it's the first chapter in this book! And I want to be clear here: this work will *never end*. **The relationships you cultivate in the first few years of your business will see you through to retirement if you let them.**

If you think I'm telling you to plan fancy dinners for your friends and supporters all the time, you're wrong. You don't have to do anything that makes you super uncomfortable or is just not "you." If this doesn't come naturally to you, no worries! The "work" of building relationships can be incredibly simple and easy. Start by:
- Sending one text message every day to someone to check in. Not to ask them for anything, not with any agenda. Just to say hello and that you hope they're having a great week. That's it.
- Offer to help, even if there's nothing in it for you. Do this for people you know well and people you might not know at all. You never know where this might lead you and how those connections might help you along your way.

- Write thank-you notes by hand. Send cards just to say hello. Never underestimate the power of a card or letter in the mail!
- Speak about other people carefully. Show people you are respectful and trustworthy. You'll be amazed at how that will strengthen your relationships with the people in your life, and how they'll be the first to come to your defense or help you when you need it because they know you aren't going to be two-faced behind their back.

You'll notice that you can start this relationship-building "work" today. You don't need a big business idea or a degree in your hand to put yourself on the right track for building your empire. **Get intentional with building relationships and you'll see immediate returns.** And when you do open the doors to your business, whether in person or online, you'll be amazed at the supportive people who come out to cheer you on as a result.

SOCIAL MEDIA

I can't have a chapter about building relationships as an entrepreneur without talking about social media, right?

We'll talk a lot more about social media as it pertains to business throughout the book, but for now let's focus on its role in relationship building.

You might have picked up this book because you know me from my social media presence, so it won't surprise you to hear that I think social media is an amazing tool to build relationships (and in turn, your business!). One of my closest relationships is with a woman named Becky, who I met years ago through Snapchat. Snapchat! She followed me and would message me; we began chatting pretty regularly, and eventually she talked me into doing business consulting for her company, Movéo Fit Co, which was launching in four months. I talk to her literally every day now—she is one of my very best friends and wrote the foreword in this book!

When I think about the "magic" of social media, for me it's the ability to easily find and make relationships with people like me.

Get intentional with
BUILDING RELATIONSHIPS
AND YOU'LL SEE
IMMEDIATE RETURNS.

If I want to find other female entrepreneurs, I can search the hashtag #womeninbusinessworkshop, and suddenly my feed is full of like-minded, like-motivated women. No need to tend bar, drive golf carts, or wait tables like I did back in the day, right?

Sort of. While I'm the first person to encourage people to start building and maintaining relationships on social media, I am also the first person to cringe when I see people approaching social media from a "me first" mentality.

Here's what I mean. Hop over to my Instagram feed and you'll see lots of pictures of me doing my thing. I'm making comments about my life and perspective with no expectations from my followers. Just a picture, some words, and that's it.

Now don't get me wrong—I love to engage with people who comment on my posts. I always make an effort to respond to each comment, even if it's just a simple "Thank you!" to anyone who gives me positive feedback. (See what I mean about the power of a quick thank-you?!) But I'm not selling anything on my page.

But wait a second! you might be thinking. *I see you posting about your new products for your business on social media. That's selling something, isn't it?*

Not really. Because I'm so conscious of relationships first, when you see me posting about a new product I have available, I'm not doing it to make a sale. I'm just letting people in on what's going on with me, and I get so genuinely excited I can't help but share. If they buy my new product, great. If not, that's great too. Maybe they will another time. **Maybe my stuff will never be right for them, but they feel connected to me and my brand, so they might recommend my products to someone they would be right for.**

See what I mean here? I often see people on social media rushing a sale. They create an account, post a couple times, then go full-court press getting people to buy whatever it is they're selling. Then they freak out when they don't get instant results—or worse, they get so caught up in followers and likes that they grow inauthentic and have what I like to call a "social media identity crisis." They mimic others, post things for the wrong reasons, get highly emotional, start the comparison game, attack "competition" (or what they deem as competition), and don't have any sort of plan of action. They're thirsty for attention, and it shows.

That's not a relationships-first mentality, and it will bite you in the ass if you're not careful.

The trick with social media is to be *intentional*. Everyone loves using that word nowadays, but it's true. Make a plan to take who you are and how you can be helpful to other people, and think of how you can do that on social media for the long term.

And be patient. Relationships take time to build. Remember that the next time you're envious of someone's social media profile! And keep in mind that engagement—*relationship*—is the goal here. I'd rather have a hundred engaged followers than a million bots, and so should you.

I started my entire business on social media. Back in 2013, I started a free Facebook group where I would post healthy recipes. I had about twelve followers when I started. Soon, it started to grow. Then Snapchat became the next big thing. I left Facebook for the most part and started using Snapchat daily. Because I created solid relationships with my Facebook followers, they followed me there. They were genuinely excited to get to see what I was up to in real time.

During this time, I was writing my first cookbook, and I leveraged Snapchat to begin to build more relationships and my brand as a whole. Every day I would do what I dubbed a "Snaptorial" (think of it as a tutorial on Snapchat). I would pop on and show a new recipe every single day for about fourteen months. I became the go-to for people looking for healthy recipes. People would share my page with friends, then those friends brought more friends; it was a snowball effect.

All because I'd had the patience to grow a real following of supporters.

The best part is that I made so many new friends, many of whom I still have to this day!

Three years after starting my Snaptorials, I published my cookbook. It was my first book, and I really had no idea what to expect.

The outpouring of support was beyond my wildest dreams. I had built so many solid relationships through the years that my book immediately became a bestseller, and before I had a chance to catch my breath, I had to place an order for another print run because I'd sold out! All thanks to the amazing people I had met over the years.

They made my book a bestseller.

They sent their friends.

They recommended me to others.

RELATIONSHIPS FIRST AT WORK

Let's say you've already figured this stuff out and have a business you're running. (Congratulations on your success, by the way!) Relationships are *still* your first priority.

Once you start bringing employees into the mix, it's important that they are also adopting this same relationships-first mentality. That's why I have my core values printed and hanging on the wall of my headquarters, so everyone can see them and be reminded of them. They're a constant reminder that we're all doing this together, even if our job roles are all different.

Here's what this looks like for me, with my employees:

- If anyone is "hard selling" on my team, I remind them that that's not what we're all about. Put all that hard-selling energy into creating real, trusting relationships with people.
- It is so important to us to include a handwritten thank-you note with every single purchase at The Paper & Plan. That's right. Every single one. And yes, I practice what I preach!
- My team and I carefully cultivate our email list. Social media platforms come and go, but that email list is essential for keeping your relationships and connections with your customers. I always ask the one-on-one coaching clients I work with, "If social media died tomorrow, how would you reach your customers?" The answer is email marketing.
- I, along with everyone on my team, genuinely care about our customers' experience. We welcome feedback, even if it's not positive. If someone wants to return a product for any reason, I want their experience with my staff and me to be positive no matter the circumstance.

- I listen more than I speak. This is a good habit to get into in life, but you can start out with your business. People love telling stories about their lives—listen to them! Doing this creates a better work environment for your team and a better experience for your customers. Mind you, it's just not storytelling—it's them telling you what matters to them. And if you listen, you'll know how to serve them better!

Of course, none of this matters if you don't have a great product that you can stand behind. We'll talk about that in the next chapter, but it's true what they say about not being able to polish a turd. Your product—no matter what it is—needs to be your best work.

But trust me when I say that **a relationships-first mentality is going to make it so your product is your best work.** When you're carefully creating real, authentic relationships, you will inevitably be more in tune with what your customers want. You won't have to worry that your ideas aren't worthwhile—you'll be so connected with your customers that you'll *know* what ideas are going to resonate with them.

I feel lucky I got to learn this at a young age, but you're never too old to cultivate this mindset as an entrepreneur. The relationships you create will be the wind in your sails as you grow, create, and succeed in your business.

2
MAKE
IT YOUR BEST WORK

REMEMBER WHEN YOU WERE A KID and would take a couple dollars to the Dollar Store, so excited to buy something for yourself? Maybe it was some off-brand jelly beans, or maybe it was a toy or a box of crayons. It didn't matter. You just were excited to get something new.

And then you came home and tasted your wax-like candy, played with your weird-smelling plastic toy, or tried to color in your coloring book with anemic crayons. Within seconds, you realized your mistake.

The crap they sold you only cost a dollar for a reason. It was *crap*.

I was fortunate that my parents instilled in me at an early age that you get what you pay for. They didn't "reward" me with a trip to the Dollar Store to buy junk; they encouraged me to earn money for and create things of value. I'll never forget making those Western-style concho keychains that were all the rage back in the day. (Remember those? The big silver-metal buckle with colorful leather strips stacked with colorful beads?) I was only about nine years old, but my parents were so proud to see their daughter practicing the entrepreneurial spirit they wanted to foster in me. So when I asked my dad if I could send them to his office to sell, I was so excited when he said yes! I immediately went to work on a little box set-up to display them properly. I started with standard keychains, and soon started taking custom orders. I was overjoyed that these big-time, important adults liked *my* product!

My parents did more than just protect me from making poor shopping decisions with their example. They showed me that anything I did in life, from the crafts I made to the way I spoke and carried myself, was a **direct reflection of my character and my standards.** If I was constantly cutting corners, doing just "okay" work in school, it didn't matter what I *told* people I valued. In fact, what I said I valued didn't matter at all. People could see what I valued by the way I conducted myself on a daily basis. As the ever popular (and true) saying goes: *Actions speak louder than words.*

I'm not going to say I've never been tempted to cut corners. I'm human, after all, and far from perfect. I bought my first home when I was nineteen, and to say it needed work would be the understatement of the century. I was so excited to renovate and make it mine. I saw all the things I wanted it to have in my mind. I didn't recognize that, because I had never lived anywhere other than with my parents, I had zero idea how much building supplies, appliances, and decor cost.

Yikes! Talk about sticker shock.

To do my best to defray the cost, I did all the projects as cheaply as possible. If you've ever renovated anything before, you know that doing things on the cheap can end up being more expensive and wasteful in the long run. That's exactly what happened to me. I vowed never to make that mistake again and to save until I could do it the right way.

Entrepreneurs and leaders of all kinds, listen up. After getting into the "relationships first" mindset, you're going to be so excited to share your idea with the world. I love the enthusiasm. But trust me when I say you do *not* want to be the Dollar Store version of your product or service. Just like in your relationships, you'll be far happier in the long run with one or two quality products than with a bunch of shit you can't stand behind. If you go that route, you'll end up embarrassing yourself and building a bad reputation.

Make it your best work.

Make it your BEST WORK.

QUALITY, NOT QUANTITY

We say "quality over quantity" so much nowadays that the phrase has almost lost its meaning. And frankly, I have seen woo-woo social media "influencers" talking about "quality over quantity" while practicing the exact opposite in their own businesses. This is *not* the way, I promise you that.

Engrave the phrase "built to last" in your brain. Model your products (and services) with those three little words in mind.

"Built to last" is another way of saying "I love this, and have put so much care into this product because I know you will love it, too."

Before you start making your business plans, leasing office space, and taking out loans for your great big badass idea, keep this in mind first. It's been said so many times by so many great people, and yet I find myself *constantly* repeating it when I coach entrepreneurs:

***Quality* is the best business plan.**

I'm going to keep saying it until it sinks in.

Quality. Is. The. Best. Business. Plan.

Here's the deal. When I opened my flower shop, I knew I was in competition with a bunch of other flower shops and gift shops in the area. Flowers and gifts aren't exactly brand-new, groundbreaking ideas no one has ever thought of before.

So how was I going to make myself and my work stand out?

I had two options:

1. I could do as much business as possible. I could buy as many flowers, vases, and Dollar Store–type gifts as cheaply as I could and spend my time figuring out how to beat the prices of my competition. Or . . .
2. I could spend my time figuring out how to make my flower shop offer the very best products. I wouldn't be the cheapest option in town, but my products and services would be the absolute best. I would be known for being the highest-quality, most unique destination flower shop around.

You can guess which option I went for.

QUALITY
IS THE BEST BUSINESS PLAN.

I'm not saying you won't find short-term success doing things the faster, easier, and cheaper way. But here's what I knew as I sought out handcrafted items for my gift shop and made relationships with quality vendors in my state to fill my flower shop with custom, unique items that no one could find anywhere else: I might be selling less product, but **I would be selling to the right buyer**... and the right buyers are friends with other right buyers... see what happens here? *Growth!* Customers who valued quality over quantity would come back time and time again because they knew that what I offered was going to be superior.

If you're one of those entrepreneur types with a million great ideas, keep in mind that you might have to rein in your enthusiasm. I once worked with a woman who could clearly see the end result of her product: a bestselling book, a podcast, an empire! Again, I love the enthusiasm, but we're focused on quality here, right? She had a demanding full-time job, a big family, kids in sports—all of it. I knew there was no way she could do it all right out of the gate. I advised her to start with a podcast, which was something she could do with minimal time and investment, getting off the ground quickly and beginning to build her personal brand on this platform that would serve her as she grew to share and promote her next endeavor. Then she could focus on growing her following, and while all that was going, she could begin drafting her book and all the projects that would come after.

Could she have found a way to do it all at once? Maybe. But she and I both knew it wouldn't be her best work in every capacity. **Patience always pays off.**

You already know that a relationships-first mindset is the first stepping-stone in successful entrepreneurship. **The simple truth is that I was able to build relationships simply by presenting my business and product in the same way I presented myself: as the very best I could possibly provide.**

I feel like I need to insert a little note here that by "presentation" I don't mean physical appearance—I mean how you carry yourself, how you express your confidence, how you respond and react, and how you treat others. First impressions do matter—I remember being told when I was around sixteen years old, "You never know at what moment in life you will meet your next boss, partner, customer. If you meet them today, what would they say?" That always stuck with me.

I *led* with that, and still do.

The simple truth is that
I WAS ALWAYS ABLE TO BUILD RELATIONSHIPS
SIMPLY BY PRESENTING MY BUSINESS
AND PRODUCT IN THE SAME WAY
I PRESENTED MYSELF: **AS THE VERY
BEST I COULD POSSIBLY PROVIDE.**

QUALITY OVER QUANTITY IN PRACTICE

Okay, so what if you don't have a flower shop? What if your big badass idea has nothing to do with finding people in a different part of your state who handmake their own soap, weave their own baskets, and handcraft their own beautiful linen sprays? (Those sprays were *amazing,* you guys!)

Simple. You get in the mind of your ideal client. You look at the product or service you are selling and ask yourself three questions:

1. **Is this my very best work?** (No? Stop everything you're doing and make it better.)
2. **Would I pay for this product or service?** (No? What would you change so you *would* pay for it?)
3. **What is the *real* value of this product or service?** (No "real" value? Go back to the drawing board and figure out what that is.)

Entrepreneurs can get into a mindset where they chase the high of making quick money and tons of sales. They're so caught up in getting their products or services out there and turning a profit that they cut corners thinking no one will notice, spend money where they don't need to, and end up putting out ten shitty products when they really only had one product that was of any real value.

And guess what? Those nine shitty products they put out there end up sinking the entire ship.

Long after I sold the flower shop, as I created The Paper & Plan Co, I kept this quality-over-quantity mentality at the forefront, and I still do. When I started out, I didn't have a huge line of stationery and other paper products. I started with one thing: planners. And I made those planners the best, most quality product I possibly could.

I sold those planners for two years, carefully watching the reactions, reading the comments, accepting feedback, and (of course) creating and curating my relationships. Did I sell less than I could have at the time?

Maybe. But I wouldn't have had it any other way. Patience pays off, and now we are known for our attention to quality, delivering a great experience, and helpful customer service.

You want that too. Especially if you're in this for the long haul.

IMAGE IS EVERYTHING

You've heard it a million times:

It's not what's on the outside but what's on the inside that counts!

That might be true when it comes to some things, but when it comes to your product, the thing you want other people to purchase from you using *their hard-earned money?*

That shit had better be your best work. And it should *show* that it's your best work, inside *and* out!

Let's go back to chapter 1, because again, this goes back to **the power of relationships.** Entrepreneurs will launch a product or service before they're ready, get distracted by making a big sale, and then get confused why those sales aren't sustainable.

I don't know how to make this more clear:

"Good enough" is a slogan for the lazy.

If you're creating a product or a service that is "good enough," you're not creating any brand loyalty. You're operating on a single-sale mentality. That's it.

"Good enough"
IS A SLOGAN FOR
THE LAZY.

And let me be honest here: this isn't just about your product. It's about your image. Remember the beginning of this chapter, when I was talking about how my parents modeled to me the importance of presenting the best version of myself? How that image was much more than just how I looked—it was an expression of what people could expect from me and the quality of my work.

This translates directly into a successful D-to-C (direct-to-customer) business.

I'll explain what I mean. Go to Amazon right now and type "planner" in the search bar. Go ahead, do it. You'll get hundreds if not thousands of options, all of which you can buy with a couple clicks. A few days later, you'll get a box or one of those mustard-yellow envelopes thrown on your doorstep, with your planner inside and nothing else.

There will be no joy from that purchase. And I promise you you'll be underwhelmed by the product you receive.

That is the exact opposite of the experience I want to create for my customers, and it should be for you too. We wrap each and every product with a branded band and sticker seal, carefully place it in a crisp glassine bag, wrap the entire purchase in tissue paper, and seal it with a branded sticker. We write a handwritten note to the customer. We carefully select beautiful custom shipping boxes and think about the presentation of the package down to the finest detail. I don't say this to brag at all—I say this to stress the importance of your details and care for each order. Lord knows I don't do this because it's easier. I do it because I want the products I ship out to my customers to be our very best work, every time.

The way I see it, I don't compete with Amazon or any other stationery business that cuts corners and provides a cheap product. If someone wants to spend their money that way, that's fine. But I know how I want to lead my life and my business, and I know that presenting my business and product a certain way will also attract the kind of customer that aligns with my work, my message, and appreciation for the quality I strive for.

This means that I have repeat customers. I have customers tagging me on social media with their purchases from my company. I'm delighting my customers and providing real value, not just cashing a paycheck. Simply put: it's all about resting your head after a long day and feeling wholeheartedly good about your day.

You attract what you put out there. It's true in life and in business.

YOU ATTRACT
what you put out there.
IT'S TRUE IN LIFE AND IN BUSINESS.

BEYOND JUST YOU

You know I want nothing to do with the fake-ass woo-woo "sprinkle it with love" bullshit that seems to infest society like hungry mosquitos on a humid July night, but I will say this: the pride I have in my product and presentation goes beyond me or even my customers. From a business standpoint, I see it this way:

As an entrepreneur, I have an opportunity and obligation to create a life and experience for many people. Not just my customers, but my suppliers and employees. So do you.

Let me explain what I mean.

I remember walking into a local restaurant several years ago. The host station was buzzing with chatter from the employees gathered there. They never looked my way or acknowledged anyone had walked in. I had to interrupt them to get a table for my friend and me. They huffed and looked annoyed, before one of the girls finally grabbed a couple menus and asked us to follow her to get seated.

We sat down at the table, which was still sprinkled with crumbs from the previous diners. The waiter came over and introduced himself, and I kindly asked that the table be wiped off. Looking irritated, he said, "Sure," in an agitated tone. He came back, wiped it down, asked for our drink orders, and a few moments later requested our food order. We ate and drank, but the wait staff would never clear our glasses or plates as we dined. They just let them collect, all while we watched them goof off. The whole experience was the exact opposite of what you would want to experience while dining.

As a customer, I was annoyed. As a business owner, I was intrigued. What was going on here?

I figured out the root cause once the general manager walked out of the back office to speak to a table next to us. They had an issue with their meal and were complaining about the service. He was condescending and refused to take any responsibility for the bad hospitality. After some back-and-forth, he threw his hands up as if to say, "What do you want me to do about it?"

I knew at that moment this guy, this "leader," was the problem. The unhelpful, rude staff were simply mimicking his poor attitude and behavior toward how to conduct business. I knew then and there that the restaurant had no future. I certainly would never be back.

Here's what I know from my experience as an entrepreneur (and human being):

- When you are a good leader, it creates a domino effect in your organization. People will follow your example, not just your words.
- A good leader creates a good culture. There's a lot of talk about work culture nowadays, and for good reason. The culture you create will make or break your business.
- A good culture leads to happy and driven employees. Happy, driven employees stick around and are motivated to do their best work every day.
- Happy and driven employees lead to happy customers—customers who want to come back time and again because they trust your business and want to see it succeed.
- Happy customers equal a great experience and great word of mouth. Word of mouth is always the best marketing.

All of which equals more sales! You can't afford to be a shitty leader. *Literally!*

The way I look at it, I am creating livelihoods for people. From the companies I source materials from to my team in the office fulfilling orders, I'm responsible for and have the opportunity to influence people's happiness.

So as you think about your best work, I want you to think beyond your product and beyond your presentation. **Your business itself also needs to be your best work.** That might mean spending more money on a smaller, higher-quality supplier. It may mean higher rent at a more desirable location for your employees.

But before you freak out that this is too much pressure or work for you, remember that if you're putting relationships first and focused on providing your highest-quality product or service, your choices are going to become smaller and more curated. You won't feel overwhelmed with options, because when you're focused on quality over quantity, you will have less to choose from once the crap you don't want anyway is taken off the list.

YOUR BEST WORK IN LEADERSHIP

There are a billion, maybe a gazillion leadership books out there, all filled with a bunch of BS about how good leaders do this, this, and this.

Let me spare you a bunch of time and energy and tell you all you need to know about being a leader:

Leadership isn't just what you do. It's who you are.

Look, we've all had shitty bosses before. If you're one of the lucky few who hasn't, maybe you've had a shitty teacher or maybe even a shitty parent. Someone with a "do as I say, not as I do" mentality.

This should be really obvious by this point: **what you say and what you do had better *match* if you want to be a successful entrepreneur.**

- If you want a team that is punctual and organized, you'd better be punctual and organized.
- If you want a team that values customer service, you'd better always provide excellent customer service.
- If you want your storefront to look and feel a certain way, you'd better present yourself in a way that matches that expectation.
- If you have high standards for your employees, you'd better have high standards for yourself.
- If you want a team that embodies and lives your core values—then you'd better embody and live them.

The list goes on. And if this feels like a lot of high-level, unmeasurable stuff that you'll figure out *after* you get your business going, let me tell you that what you model as a leader starts from day one.

I'm talking about everything. From how you answer the phone to how you shake a person's hand to how you take out the *freaking garbage*. Do all things with the highest level of care and integrity, and you'll create the business you want through your example alone.

LEADERSHIP ISN'T just what you do.
IT'S WHO YOU ARE.

THE B WORD

Entrepreneurs, especially those just starting out, use the words "branding" and "marketing" interchangeably.

They are not interchangeable.

Branding is the giving of information and value.

Marketing is an ask (for a sale).

Branding is the *push;* marketing is the *pull.*

We'll talk about this more when we talk about acting with honesty and integrity, but for now I want to focus on how branding (aka the way you put yourself out there) is so important to your ultimate success.

Years ago, I signed up for a subscription box service. It would arrive each month full of goodies for my office. Their advertisement online looked amazing. They had branded themselves as *the* subscription box for top-quality office supplies. As someone who is very visual, I loved the beautiful aesthetic of their Instagram feed. I saw some unboxing videos, and the box was carefully and meticulously curated. It had clean lines, pretty tissue paper, a matching tissue seal, and a fun pop of color. I thought to myself, *Wow, this is beautifully done!* I couldn't wait for my first shipment.

Then I opened my first box. I was shocked. There was printed text on the inside of the box, littered with misspellings and typos. The presentation was nothing like what had been shown in their advertising. The office products I had been looking forward to receiving were something I could have gotten at the Dollar Store for a few bucks. The "handwritten" thank-you card was preprinted (poorly) to look like it had been done by hand.

I was so disappointed. The branding was what had sucked me in and gotten me excited, but this was nothing like what I'd been promised. I kept thinking this was a perfect example of something that belonged in an *Instagram versus Reality* mashup.

I see this sort of thing happening all the time, and it drives me nuts. This company went so heavy on their branding, and no doubt—that branding was absolutely someone's best work! **But that's as far as their best work went.** I quickly canceled my subscription and got my money back.

I get that it can be easy to get caught up in branding. After all, "branding" is everyone's favorite buzzword on social media, with all the beautifully curated photos, posh and perfect filters, and aesthetic everything down to the damn triangle fold on the toilet paper roll. My advice: slow your roll for a bit. Getting caught up in branding and image is the same temptation we can have as entrepreneurs when we chase a quick sale. But the truth is that being thoughtful and intentional about your brand is going to pay off for you in the long run.

Here's what I mean. Let me give you an example of one of my Facebook posts back when I was first beginning to build my relationships and brand:

Coconut Oil: Nature's Secret Weapon
So you've been hearing a lot of hype about coconut oil lately, but you either (a) haven't quite bought into it or (b) aren't quite sure how to get the most benefit from it. Well, I have compiled a list of the many benefits of coconut oil and how it can become a natural and organic substitute for many of your daily health and household needs.

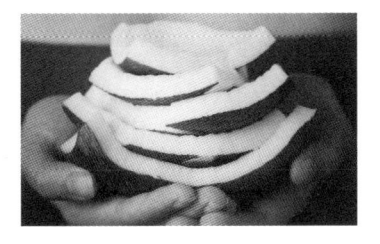

1) Cooking, frying, and baking
2) Substitute for butter
3) Substitute for vegetable oil
4) Coffee creamer
5) Moisturizer for your skin—helps with psoriasis and eczema
6) Natural SPF4 Sunscreen
7) Mix with sugar for a natural way to exfoliate skin
8) Oil pulling
9) Natural shave cream and aftershave lotion
10) Anti-bacterial skin cream
11) Reduce the itch of mosquito bites, poison ivy, and chickenpox
12) Mix with salt to exfoliate your feet
13) Eye makeup remover

SLOW AND STEADY DOES WIN THE RACE, even though as entrepreneurs we never really reach the finish line... **WE JUST MOVE FURTHER FROM THE STARTING LINE.**

Let me point out something really important here: At this point in my brand-building process, I wasn't spending a dime on Facebook ads or graphic designers. **I was just putting the best version of myself out there, knowing that if I did I would attract the following I was hoping for.**

Over time, I gained a handful of highly engaged followers. Then they shared and told a few friends, who told a few friends . . . you guessed it. Good old-fashioned word of mouth recommendations for the win.

Did I start spending money on marketing? Eventually. But only when I had the data to support what I was doing. I learned over time that Facebook was a great platform for me, and I knew my supporters there were eager for more content, so I spent money knowing I was likely to get a good return on my investment.

Again, this is not rocket science. Building my brand took time and patience, but if I wanted it to be my best work, I knew I would have to take it slowly. **Slow and steady does win the race, even though as entrepreneurs we never really reach the finish line . . . we just move further from the starting line.**

YOUR BEST WORK

Okay, so let's say you've gotten to this point and you're all in. Great. You know I'm not going to give you a bunch of "now go do a good job" BS—instead I'm going to give you a few ideas to keep you accountable.

Six ways to make sure you're always making it your best work:

1. **Focus on your customer's experience.** I mean it. In all aspects of your business, you should want to make it so your end user is delighted with their experience and glad they decided to spend their hard-earned money with you. That way, you'll have customers for life.
2. **Take your time putting systems in place.** Be patient! Find the best vendors, the best platforms, the best of everything so you can make your product or service the best it can be.
3. **Follow up.** Yep, we're going back to relationship building here, but it's also related to putting forth your best work. Are you requesting feedback from your customers? Do you have email sequencing in place to keep in contact with them?
4. **Be real.** Don't stress about messing up—you will. People love authentic connections with real human beings, so own it when you make a mistake. People are far more forgiving than you realize—this not only builds trust, but builds respect.
5. **Avoid negativity.** Putting your best work forward does not require that you put down another person's work or service. Let your product speak for itself.

6. **Be flexible.** So your plan isn't working out for some reason . . . now what? Before you freak out and cut your losses, calm yourself and think logically about what the problem might be. My husband often says, "Either you haven't worked the plan long enough or you're working the wrong plan." If your product or service needs fine tuning, do that. If you're getting feedback from the wrong people, find someone who's been in the trenches before, understands you and your customers, and isn't afraid to give you brutally honest feedback.

Again, much of what I'm recommending here is common sense when you really think about it. But it can be easy to lose sight of that if you're letting yourself get impatient and focused on a quick buck as opposed to a long-term business plan.

BUSINESS IS PERSONAL

Of course, I would be lying if I said that this is strictly unemotional work. As someone who has invested a huge amount of emotion into forming the right relationships and putting in the work to maintain them, I get it! Having the entrepreneurial mindset means you don't have the luxury of clocking in and out depending on someone else for everything. It's all you, and that can feel like a lot sometimes.

But I would argue that this is liberating too. If you get that business is personal, and if you get that you are a direct reflection of your product or service, that means that you have the opportunity to create the experience that you truly want.

That starts with making it—*all of it*—your best work.

3
PERSONAL ACCOUNTABILITY

LET'S START WITH some definitions here, shall we?

Accountability: ac·count·abil·i·ty | \ ə-kaun-tə-bi-lə-tē
- The quality or state of being accountable
- especially: an obligation or willingness to accept responsibility or to account for one's actions

Notice that nowhere does this definition say anything about admitting ultimate defeat or failure. Notice that it does not in any way imply that you are less than or incapable of being successful.

You don't suck, okay? (That's about as woo-woo as I'm willing to get in this book.)

There are two types of accountability: accountability to yourself and accountability to the people around you. For an entrepreneur, both are equally important. That's a lot of responsibility, and you'd better not ever screw it up.

I'm kidding.

The truth is that you are going to screw up from time to time in big and small ways! In those moments, you're going to have two choices:
- Lie, defer, deflect, and do anything possible to avoid the conflict or problem. Just keep on kicking that can down the road so no one ever needs to know that you are a human being capable of making mistakes. Or . . .
- Take responsibility. Look objectively at what happened and make a plan to fix it so it doesn't happen again.

You can guess which option I'm going to recommend.

Look, you have shit. You have weaknesses and blind spots, just like I do. You're not always going to nail everything, and that's okay. Believe it or not, the most successful entrepreneurs are human beings, just like you. Don't be fooled by social media or anything else that might paint a picture of everything being perfect all the time. It isn't. **The entrepreneurs who make it are the ones who aren't afraid of admitting their mistakes and taking ownership for the entire operation, not just the stuff that goes right.**

THE ENTREPRENEURS WHO MAKE IT

are the ones who aren't afraid of **ADMITTING** THEIR MISTAKES AND **TAKING** OWNERSHIP FOR THE ENTIRE OPERATION, *not just the stuff that goes right.*

For me, **accountability and responsibility are one and the same**. And you don't need a dictionary to help you define or live it as one of your core values as an entrepreneur.

ACCOUNTABILITY FROM DAY ONE

I keep saying this because it's true: the way you live your life on a daily basis is going to be a direct reflection of how you run your business. Being a person who takes responsibility for their actions, their impact, their successes, and their mistakes is something that begins well before your big badass idea starts to form and you start pocketing profits.

If this is still a bit of a mystery to you, go back to chapter 2 about making everything—and I mean *everything*—your best work.

Doing your best work every day does require some discipline. Think of it as setting your moral compass. Get yourself into routines and habits that will create the momentum you need to move forward on whatever path you've chosen, for both yourself and your business.

Author and speaker John C. Maxwell puts it this way: **Momentum has makers, takers, and breakers.** The moment I read those words in his book *The 5 Levels of Leadership*, I had to stop to read it again. And again. And then once more. It hit me like a ton of bricks. So brilliantly put.

So what does this mean?

Well, within the ecosystem of our businesses, we will have people that will create momentum—these are the **makers**. They keep the train on the tracks, make things happen, and accept responsibility to make everything their best work in order to contribute to the winning vision of the team and the company.

In this same ecosystem, we can have momentum **takers**. These people don't start anything, and they don't stop anything. They are like a dead fish in the river—they just go with the flow, contributing little or nothing to the organization. Basically, they simply exist, relying on everyone else to get them somewhere.

Lastly, we have the momentum **breakers**. These are the ones that hurt the culture and morale of the company. They don't execute on their tasks and keep others from the ability to execute as well.

You don't want to be a momentum breaker or taker. You want to be a maker.

For me, accountability practices are pretty simple, and are based around having five priorities in place every day.

That's it. Five things you need to do to add value every single day.

Those five things don't have to be earth-shattering. Work out. Read a chapter of a self-development style book. Write a report or an important pitch. Make a phone call. You know what you need to get done every day. The point isn't to make these things impossible to achieve—exactly the opposite. Our brains are hardwired to feel a sense of accomplishment when we complete a task, and that sense of accomplishment is going to be what builds momentum for the next day, and the next day after that.

I create planners for a living, so of course I incorporate these Top Five Priorities into my designs (business *is* personal, remember?). I know that keeping myself accountable to my Top Five Priorities every single day is one of the keys to my success, and I want that for my supporters/customers too.

Getting into accountability practices might seem awkward at first, but I'm always amazed at how quickly people adapt to the practice once it becomes a habit. You like making a to-do list and crossing it off? Congratulations! That's accountability!

Think of it this way: **Accountability is like a mirror. The practices you put in place are going to be a direct reflection on you, your team, and your values.** You are bound to produce your best work when you're holding yourself accountable to the high standards you've set.

The truth is, the majority of the population doesn't realize how *good* we are designed to feel and operate. Once you begin accountability practices, you will see how much more you achieve and how great it feels. You'll enjoy an improved overall mood, and better yet, the amount of potential you unlock within yourself will feel like a freaking freight train of positive momentum.

Your accountability practices won't hold you back—they'll propel you forward! Once that momentum gets going, it will be hard to stop.

ACCOUNTABILITY IS LIKE A MIRROR.

The practices you put in place are going to be a **DIRECT REFLECTION** ON **YOU**, YOUR **TEAM**, AND YOUR **VALUES**.

TIPS AND TRICKS

If you are a fly-by-the-seat-of-your-pants type of person and have never put accountability practices in place, don't freak out. This isn't brain surgery. It just requires you to turn off the noise for a couple minutes every morning and focus on what you need to do. That's it. Here are some tips to get you started:

1. **Stop overcommitting.** I used to be terrible at this... like *terrible*. If I were on fire, I would throw gasoline on myself to make it even worse. Too many things to do today? Add five more—you're up for the challenge! That was my old way of operation. I was one of those people who felt that, in order to be successful, I needed to have a calendar that was jam-packed every moment of every day. If that's how you run your life, stop it. I mean it. **Stop it.** Being busy is not a badge of honor. In fact, running yourself ragged at a nonstop pace is a great way to burn out and grow bitter and resentful of yourself and the people around you. (Trust me—I have been hospitalized a couple times for stress and exhaustion. Absolute burnout. I don't recommend it.) If you have a day with only two meetings, perfect. That means you can knock out your Top Five Priorities for the day, and maybe even have some extra time to take a walk with a friend or listen to a podcast by someone who inspires you.

2. **Know when you work best.** Whoever said the early bird gets the worm was full of it. I've never been impressed by folks who brag about what time they get up or go to sleep. There is actual data that shows that people have very different rhythms and internal clocks, meaning we have peaks of energy at different points of the day. The science behind this is totally fascinating! (If you really want to geek out about this and figure out how to use your personal internal clocks better, I recommend reading Daniel Pink's *When: The Scientific Secrets of Perfect Timing*.) For me, my best work times (aka "Zone of Genius") are between 10:00 a.m. and 4:00 p.m. After 4:00 p.m., my brain turns to mush for a while. Then I get another surge

of energy in the evening between 8:00 p.m. and 12:00 a.m. It might be totally different for you. Knowing your most energetic times is simply a matter of getting off the hamster wheel for a second and taking notice of your body and mind. The best thing about being an entrepreneur is that you are on your own schedule, not someone else's. Take advantage of that and make it work best for you!

3. **Check that ego.** Being accountable doesn't mean being rigid all the time. I'm not just talking about your calendar, I'm talking beyond that, into how you do things in your business. The way I see it, you've got a vision, right? You have a destination you want to get to; a goal you're working toward. *There are multiple ways of getting there.* You might think that one platform is best, or one vendor is perfect, or one business plan is set in stone; but you're only going to give yourself a heart attack if you fear being wrong so much that you refuse to think of different ways to do things. The same goes for taking responsibility for when things go wrong in general. Don't be too proud to admit that what you thought was best wasn't actually the right way. You're only human, after all.

4. **Be crystal clear on your role, expectations, and responsibilities.** This is absolutely crucial as a leader. The more you model what you expect and verbalize precisely what you expect from your partners and teams, the better off you'll be. We'll talk more about this later in the chapter.

Some of the best advice I can give to entrepreneurs just starting out and even veteran entrepreneurs is to keep this at the front of your mind at all times:

See it
Own it
Solve it
Do it

Let's break that down a bit:

> **See it:** Identify the issue.
> **Own it:** Accept responsibility even if you didn't create it.
> **Solve it:** Assess what needs to get done to course correct.
> **Do it:** Take action to correct it.

Let's show this as a super basic real-world example.

> **See it:** You see a piece of trash on the ground.
> **Own it:** You didn't put it there, but you accept responsibility for it.
> **Solve it:** You know you need to pick up the trash and find a trash can.
> **Do it:** You pick up the trash and dispose of it properly.

Got it?

Don't mistake me as meaning that you can't have any "life" outside your work. You're going to work hard, no doubt. You are going to act accountable and be accountable, and it's going to feel like a 24/7 job sometimes. But it doesn't have to be. I'm going to take this moment to again remind you that you are only human. You need your sleep, and you need your downtime.

We always hear a lot of fluff about having a healthy work/life balance. I don't know there's such a thing as "balance" as an entrepreneur, but you will have to find a *flow* that works for you. Believe it or not, having a healthy work/life flow is being accountable. To yourself. It starts and ends with *you*.

BACKWARD PLANNING

Okay, so your daily accountability practices are one thing. But what about holding yourself accountable when you're working toward a huge project with countless steps and moving pieces? And what if you have multiple huge projects to juggle at the same time?

That's the life of an entrepreneur. For me, the trick is pretty simple—I goal set and plan backward. Instead of starting from step one and working my way toward the finish line, I *start* at the finish line. Or at least I start with where I want to arrive. I start with what success looks like for that particular project, then fill in the stepping-stones it will take to get there, working backward.

Again, this isn't brain surgery. Think about it like going on a road trip. **You wouldn't get in the car without checking your route, knowing your stops, and making sure you packed appropriately. It's the same with project management.**

Setting Top Five Priorities every day helps, but for larger projects it will take a bit more thought. Here's a very simple example of what backward planning looks like for me:

18 MONTH GOAL

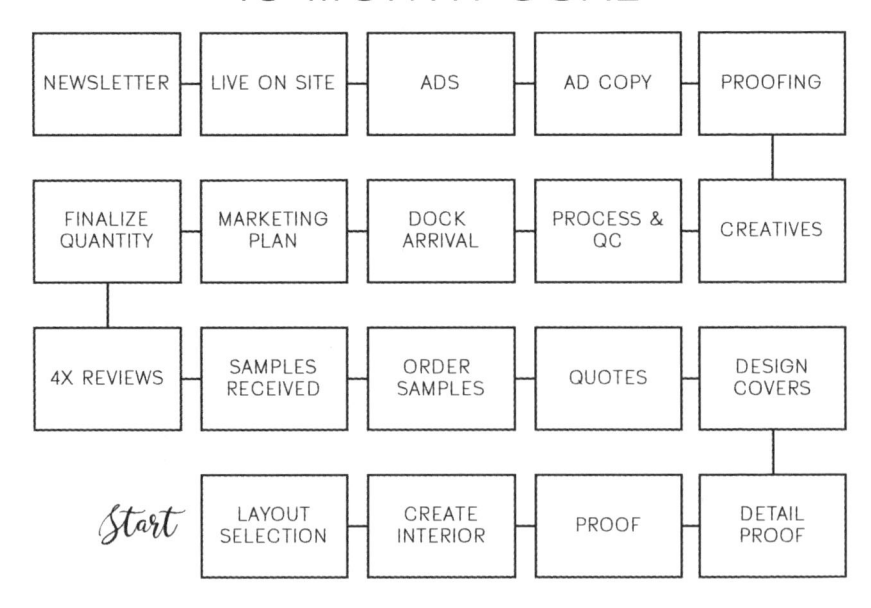

NEWSLETTER	LIVE ON SITE	ADS	AD COPY	PROOFING
FINALIZE QUANTITY	MARKETING PLAN	DOCK ARRIVAL	PROCESS & QC	CREATIVES
4X REVIEWS	SAMPLES RECEIVED	ORDER SAMPLES	QUOTES	DESIGN COVERS
Start → LAYOUT SELECTION	CREATE INTERIOR	PROOF	DETAIL PROOF

66 | RELATIONSHIPS FIRST

YOU WOULDN'T GET IN THE CAR WITHOUT checking your route, KNOWING YOUR STOPS, *and making sure you packed appropriately.* **IT'S THE SAME** FOR PROJECT MANAGEMENT.

In this example, you'll notice that I have the steps to completion laid out so they're easily digestible and clear. It's nothing fancy or terribly complicated. I've just thought through the steps needed to get to my end goal, starting from the end and working my way backward. Now I have a roadmap to get to where I want to go, and I won't be panicked or scrambling if (and when) things go off course.

It's tempting to skip this. We can get so excited about our big project or launch that we can fixate on the end result without taking the time to think through the details. Then, when the shit hits the fan, we freak out.

Look, the shit *will* hit the fan in one way or another. You know what they say about the best-laid plans, don't you? (Look it up.) Do yourself a favor and get as organized as you can for when that does happen. That way, you'll be able to fix things quickly and move forward instead of racing around in a panic.

If you know yourself well enough to recognize that even this is going to be a challenge for you, get yourself an accountability partner. Hey, it works in fitness. It works for running your own business as well. I have lots of fellow entrepreneurs I check in on all the time to ask questions about their best practices and get inspiration from. Don't confuse this with some sort of weekly #bossbabe "You can do this!" fluff. I don't do that. An accountability partner is someone who will give you the hard truth when you need to hear it, someone you respect and whose opinion matters so much to you that you're willing to listen when they have a suggestion for how your business (or even your life) can run better.

HOLDING OTHERS ACCOUNTABLE

If you work with a team, you're of course going to be modeling this for them. That's a given. Ninety percent of the time, that's going to work to keep your team on the right track.

But every so often, it won't work. You're going to have to call *other people* out on their shit. That's part of the deal being a leader too.

I remember once when a person on my team emailed me a template she'd created for a story post on Instagram. The indentations were off on one of the items. She was normally super thorough, but this was clearly not her best work. I had two options in that situation:

1. Keep quiet and just fix it myself. No biggie. She'd do better next time, right?
2. Call her out, make her aware of it, and make sure it didn't happen again.

You can guess which option I chose.

Keep in mind that we are still operating with a **relationships-first** mentality. Always. All the time. So no, I didn't run screaming to her desk and ask her just who the hell she thought she was, sending me this garbage. Save that drama for the movies.

In this particular situation, I just sent her a quick text response. "Hey, I was looking at this template you made, and it doesn't align with our core value about making everything your best work . . ." It was lighthearted, but also an important reminder to her that these core values we have are all of ours—not just mine. We hold them true, no matter how small or large an issue. It's who we are and what we stand for.

When she responded a few moments later with an updated template, she said, "I'm sorry, Emily. This is my best work now." It was. And we moved right along in our work.

You, as an entrepreneur or leader in your company, need to do the same thing. When you see something, call it out. You'll be amazed at how quickly you can nip problems in the bud while keeping harmony between your four walls. But, and I can't stress this enough, that only works if you model this behavior.

In my office, there is no job that is beneath me. There is nothing I ask of my team that I wouldn't be willing to do myself. I encourage my team to call me out if I'm not living up to one of our core values too. There's no big idea or project that I don't share with my team and let them be part of. **We're in this together. No weak links. No excuses.**

We're all in this together.
NO WEAK LINKS.
NO EXCUSES.

Again, the core values for my company aren't something that we refer to every now and then. I have them hanging on the wall of the office, as a constant reminder for *all of us*.

WHEN LIFE HAPPENS

So, you put some accountability practices in place and you're golden, right? Smooth sailing.

Wrong.

You're an entrepreneur, remember? The waters we sail on will always be choppy and unpredictable.

Even the most responsible, accountable entrepreneurs get derailed from time to time. There are several things I do when I find myself unmotivated or losing interest in my plan:

1. **I go back to the lists I made while backward planning.** Is there anything I missed? Can I identify any issues and resolve them quickly?
2. **I redo my vision boards.** There's something about creating a vision board that is really helpful to reset focus and goals.
3. **I create new marketing materials.** I'm not saying totally rebrand yourself, but a new campaign or even a social media post can help get you back on track.
4. **I quiet the noise.** It's easy to get in your own head sometimes. Go for a walk without headphones in, take a break from social media, read, or lie on the floor for five minutes and just breathe and clear your mind. We are constantly processing information; sometimes our brains need a break to reset.
5. **I schedule my good habits.** Maybe it's my favorite workout or meal to cook, or maybe it's lunch with a friend. Our brains love having something to look forward to, so I make that a part of my Top Five Priorities too.

And sometimes, even that's not going to be enough. Sometimes, life's going to throw you such a huge curveball that you're going to rethink the whole entrepreneurship thing altogether. I'm talking about the big stuff. Shit that might threaten to derail you personally or professionally. Shit you should have seen coming, and shit you have absolutely no control over.

You're going to have to model accountability then too, even if you can't imagine getting out of bed in the morning. But how?

Even I don't have a planner that's going to help you through times like that. All I can say is that I've been there. I have been in situations where life felt like too much, shit was too heavy, and I just fell to my knees. During those dark times, the only thing that pulled me through was knowing how much I was needed. I *needed* to get through it, not just for me, but for the people I loved and who depended on me. Was it hard? Hell yes, it was. I never said any of this was going to be easy.

I've found myself thinking about this a lot in the past two years when the world came to a screeching halt because of the COVID-19 pandemic. Not only did the entrepreneurs in my life (myself included) need to quickly pivot to figure out how to keep our businesses rolling, we had to do so all while balancing the needs of everyone else who depended on us, offering them security during such an unknown and unpredictable time.

The way I see it, there are two types of entrepreneurs: the ones who find themselves in scary, uncharted territory, feeling defeated and rushing to find the quickest exit route, and the ones who rise to the occasion. The ones who were born to fight, who feed off the dark and gritty work and won't back down. They're too damn stubborn to quit, even when quitting might seem easier.

That second type of entrepreneur is the kind I want you to be.

Remember: there are a lot of people who want to play this game, but few will show up for practice. **When you want to win a championship, every damn day matters.**

WHEN YOU WANT TO WIN A CHAMPIONSHIP, every damn day MATTERS.

4

RESPECT
THE POTENTIAL AND SIGNIFICANCE OF
EVERY PERSON

REMEMBER HOW I TOLD YOU in the introduction that I was a shy kid? This went beyond feeling nervous talking in front of people. I look back on that time in my life and remember having no self-confidence, no belief in myself. It's hard to describe unless you've experienced it yourself. Despite having awesome parents who set a great example for me, who constantly told me they believed in me and pointed out my gifts, I stayed in my shell for a long time.

It was Mr. Enke's tenth-grade class that really changed me. He didn't just tell me he believed in me—I'd been hearing that from people my whole life. "Believing" in people was what everyone did, right?

Mr. Enke *saw* me.

Here's what I mean by that. Mr. Enke knew my background. I was a farm girl, good at school, and easily made friends with everyone. He told me I was one of those people who always looked for the good in people. He sensed that I was hungry to learn, not just in school but about other people and their stories. He watched me naturally take on leadership positions despite my shyness.

So when he encouraged me to take on more leadership roles in the FFA, he wasn't giving me the standard "you can do it" line, the one every kid hears so much that it's lost its meaning. He actually took me aside and told me he saw that I had leadership qualities in me. He knew *from watching me* that I had more potential.

It was from that encouragement that I decided to run for chapter secretary at FFA . . . and won. And then I ran for president . . . and won. I earned award after award as a leader and speaker, and I can credit Mr. Enke for giving me the boost I needed to get there.

Thanks, Mr. Enke. :)

If you've had a Mr. Enke in your life, you know how life-changing this type of influence can be. The good news is that as an entrepreneur, you have the opportunity to pay that encouragement forward.

No, not opportunity—you have a *requirement* to pay it forward.

That's what good leaders do, and that's what successful entrepreneurs do. They see and respect the potential and significance *in everyone they interact with*.

I don't say this because I'm trying to sell you on some woo-woo work culture where everything is sunshine and rainbows. What I am saying is that I know from my own experience and the people that I coach: when you create an environment like Mr. Enke did for me, an environment where everyone you interact with feels seen, appreciated, and challenged appropriately, you are bound to be more successful in the long run. You're going to have a better product. You're going to create relationships with vendors who share your vision. You're going to have employees who want to stick with you and give their best work, day in and day out. You're going to have customers who come back for more because they trust you have their best interests at heart.

See how that translates directly into more money for you? But you don't lead with that, not ever. Relationships first.

GET FURTHER FROM THE STARTING LINE

If you haven't figured this out already, we need to start here:

You are never going to reach your "full" potential. Your potential is not a final destination, it's a constant evolution. The goal isn't to get to a finish line, it's to get further from the starting line. The same thing goes for your team, your vendors, your customers, and every other person you interact with in business (and in life!).

For me, one of my most rewarding experiences as a one-on-one business coach is helping people through their ups and downs to that next level of unlocking their potential. One client who always sticks out to me is a woman I'll call Wylie. Wylie believed in her product and her brand, but she lacked the confidence to really push them to market. She took a year to develop the product, then another six months on her branding. Now she had invested eighteen months into this product and was terrified to launch.

No doubt, there are plenty of entrepreneurs who launch too soon. They're so desperate to get their product to market but don't think through all the details, including packaging, messaging, and the first impressions of the end user. They launch, they crash, and then they burn.

Then, there are entrepreneurs like Wylie. They overthink everything to the point of paralysis. They are constantly delayed in their launch because they keep tweaking and re-tweaking the product, updating their websites constantly, and changing their minds on their branding before they even make their first sale.

If Wylie's story rings true for you, and you're looking for your "sign" to move forward, here it is: *just launch already!*

Wylie overthought so many things, which I get. We all want it to be perfect, right? However, getting tied up with perfection is really falling victim to procrastination.

After a loving come-to-Jesus meeting with her about this, Wylie finally launched. Was she fearful? Yes. Nervous? Yes. But she did it.

Want to know what happened? She absolutely killed it. The marketing was spot on, and she sold out her product in forty-eight short hours. I was so proud of her. And to be clear, she had it in her the whole time. **Sometimes it takes someone to let you know what they see in you, so you see it yourself.**

Like so many entrepreneurs, Wylie doubted her potential. She was battling negative thought patterns and a fear of rejection, something many of us can relate to.

For someone like Wylie, "Woo woo, you can do it!" platitudes weren't enough. She needed someone to lead her to the plate, even though she was terrified. She needed me to be her Mr. Enke, to insist that she stop making excuses and just take her place at bat. Once she did that, she hit a home run. She would take that confidence with her for the rest of her career.

This means a couple things as an entrepreneur:

1. **Your team is counting on you to be their Mr. Enke.** We'll talk much more about this later in the chapter, but for now I want to remind you *yet again* about the very first core value in this book—relationships first. You aren't just employing people as an entrepreneur; you're taking on an important part of their personal development. Your investment in those relationships will pay off big time in the long run.

2. **You need to be your own Mr. Enke.** Being an entrepreneur has a lot of perks, but having someone hold your hand through the ups and downs as your own personal cheerleader isn't one of them. That's why it's so crucial that you hold yourself to a high standard, not just with fluffy words on social media, but in *action*. Not sure about how this works? Go back to chapter 3, where we talked about accountability.

Look, I'm old enough to remember a time when being a "boss" had a certain expectation. Buttoned-up suits, mean tempers, the whole bit. Those times have changed (thank God). I'm not saying you won't have boundaries as a boss or leader, but what I am saying is that seeing the potential in others (and yourself) is something to be grateful you have the opportunity to do.

And it's simple, when you think about it. **It's really nothing more than watching, listening to, and acting from a place of genuinely wanting the best for the people around you.**

SEEKING FUTURE POTENTIAL

Business is personal. (Have I repeated that enough times for you yet?) Business is *personal*. And it starts with you, and how you bring people into the fold of your new enterprise.

Seeking out employees to help us bring our dreams to life is one of the most important decisions we will make as entrepreneurs. Don't hire people lightly. Trust me on this. It's a lot easier to be a Mr. Enke to people you respect and admire, not to mention a lot more financially beneficial if you can retain a solid team for the long term.

As many people have said before, we have a tendency to hire people based on what they can do. We fire them based on who they are.

What if you hired people based on who they are?

Here's how I do this. When I interview someone to be on my team, or even if I'm building a relationship with a vendor, I never ask the standard "Why do you want to work here?" "What are your strengths and weaknesses?" bullshit.

IT'S REALLY NOTHING MORE THAN watching, listening to, and acting from a place of **GENUINELY WANTING THE BEST** for the people around you.

Instead, I create real-life scenarios based on the company's core values, and just let them talk. I keep my poker face the entire time and never lead them to an answer. I just sit back and listen for them to show me their values.
- You're at the gas station pumping gas when a person who looks like they're down and out asks you for five dollars. What do you do?
- You're at the grocery store parking lot and you see several shopping carts left abandoned. What do you do?
- There's a woman with three kids at the grocery checkout line and the kids are getting restless. The mom looks frazzled and stressed. What would you do?
- You're in a rush to a meeting and just walking in when you see a few pieces of trash outside the building. What do you do?

You might be thinking I'm looking for a specific answer to these questions. I'm not. I'm actually looking for the person to simply reveal to me who they are, rather than what they can do.
- **I'm looking for honesty.** I never like it when someone tries to sell me on their goodness or perfection in an interview. I can smell a disingenuous answer a mile away. You need to be able to do this too if you want to hire top-quality people. (A book that can help you if your bullshit detector is off is called *Spy the Lie*, by Philip Houston, Michael Floyd, and Susan Carincero. It's written by former CIA agents who teach you how to detect deception.)
- **I'm looking for a quick response.** Of course, we'd all love ten minutes to think and curate the "best" answer to every interview question. But that's not a luxury life affords us. I want to see that the person is quick on their feet and secure in who they are. Confidence is always a good trait.
- **I'm looking for agility.** I don't care what sort of business you're starting—you're going to need to have a staff of people around you who can quickly pivot if (not if, *when*) things don't go according to plan. If I get an answer from someone that feels rehearsed or too easy, I throw them a quick curveball to make sure they are quick on their feet under pressure.

- **I'm looking for what makes them unique.** Most importantly, how I can use their unique strengths and weaknesses to see and understand their potential. For example, if someone comes into an interview to work for me and is clearly very creative (maybe I can see it in the way they dress or the way they express themselves), then I'm actively thinking about where they would fit best on my team and where I could allow them to let their creativity really flourish. More than once, I've interviewed someone for a certain position only to offer them a different position because I could see they had much more opportunity for growth there.

See what I mean? **I'm not just seeking out what they can do for me. I'm seeking out what I can do for them and how I can help them grow.**

To be clear, this isn't just a strategy I use when hiring staff. I use it when I'm developing relationships with my vendors too. Anyone can give me a checklist of payment terms; what I'm looking for is a vendor who shares my values and work ethic.

And yes, I'm looking to surround myself with people who will take calculated risks and want to develop themselves and their skills. This is one of the best parts of owning your own business—being able to vet people based on who they are, not just what they can give you. I learn from them just as much as they learn from me. It's served me well in business *and* in life.

Wait, Emily, I can hear you asking. *Isn't there a danger in hiring people like this? What if you see and respect their potential so much that they end up leaving you to go on to bigger and better things?*

Of course that's going to happen. And that is an awesome thing! It would be incredibly selfish of me to want to bring people into my business only to keep them chained there for life. On many occasions I've told my employees that I *hope* they outgrow me. I *want* to see them move on and build their dreams, and I *want* them to always look back on their time with me as a crucial, positive part of their growth.

This all goes back to the *requirement* you have to seek out and respect the potential of the people you do business with. Yes, my expectations are high. Yours should be too. I have no interest in people trying to sell me on the fact that they're a hard worker. It should be a given that you're a hard worker! Working people hard isn't the holy grail of entrepreneurship.

Relationships are the holy grail of entrepreneurship.

RELATIONSHIPS ARE THE HOLY GRAIL of entrepreneurship.

And don't think this practice of seeing and valuing potential in others doesn't apply to your customers—it does! You obviously won't be interviewing your customers to see if they match with your values, but when you practice this mindset of looking at and seeing the whole person and developing relationships with them, then you're naturally going to attract the right customers to your business.

Take one look at my Instagram and you'll see what I mean. I make planners, remember? My business is to make people's lives easier. Social media has been a great way for me to "see" my customers and value them. I listen to feedback, incorporate it into future projects, and feel genuine satisfaction when I know that my work has helped someone else do *their* work better.

Respecting the potential in others is an endless cycle, really. And the truth is, I wouldn't want there to be a final destination. It's one of the most fun parts of the journey as an entrepreneur.

RESPECTING POTENTIAL IN PRACTICE

Raise your hand if you've ever worked for a shitty boss. Your hand is up, isn't it?

What made them shitty?

Chances are they weren't bad at the work they did. They wouldn't have been promoted if they sucked at their job, right?

No, they probably did pretty well at their job. What they didn't do well was the interpersonal stuff. Maybe they were a loose cannon at work, always emotional and unpredictable in their expectations or behavior. Maybe they micromanaged everyone on the team to death and stifled any individual expression or creativity. Maybe they absolutely sucked at giving constructive feedback.

Bad management is like a cancer in your team, and the cancer will grow and spread quicker than you think. Ever just walked into a building and felt that the energy was just . . . off? You could just tell everyone hates to work there? You don't want that.

"So what?" I can hear some people saying. "I'm not giving people jobs to make friends or create some sort of fluffy, froufrou environment. I'm paying them to do their best work."

Wrong. *Relationships first.*

Like I said, I would never in a million years tell you to create some sort of happy-go-lucky, fake-positivity work environment. That's not at all what I mean by respecting the potential in others.

What I mean is that people aren't robots. Everyone wants to feel seen and valued. People will do their best work in an environment where they feel respected and challenged. And maybe most importantly, your employees will stay with you much longer if they feel these things consistently.

If this feels like some sort of big and scary thing that you don't have time for with all the other shit you have to manage as a business owner, calm down. Again, none of this is brain surgery. It's actually really simple when you stop to think of it in terms of the Golden Rule of treating others the way you'd want to be treated.

- **Listen.** I am constantly amazed by the number of people whose egos are so inflated that they think their voice is the only one in the room that matters. Respecting potential in others and seeing their significance is as simple as shutting up and letting other people talk, think, and express themselves.
- **Ask questions.** I have developed a habit of asking my team if there's anything I can do or that they need to make their jobs easier or more efficient. Sometimes they say, "Nope, we're good," but sometimes they'll ask for something specific, something I can provide, something I had no idea would make the business run more smoothly. So simple.
- **Have clear boundaries.** Whew, this is important. My teams and I have great working relationships. I know a bit about their lives, and they know a bit about mine. We joke and have a great time.

But that doesn't mean that I allow any of the lines between business and personal to blur, especially in the age of social media. Everyone has different definitions of what they're comfortable with, and that's fine. The trick is to know *your* comfort level and maintain clear boundaries at all times.

Shit happens, of course. That's life. That's why I always suggest to entrepreneurs that they should create a circle of people around them whom they respect and admire, people living the life and running the type of business they want to have. Turn to them when you need clarity and perspective. Just be careful—with social media, there's a lot of shysters out there who want to sell an image and lifestyle that is fake as hell. Consider yourself warned, and choose wisely.

YOUR CORE VALUES, AGAIN

Seeing and respecting the potential and significance in everyone is something that should be ingrained in you as an entrepreneur . . . and as a human being! And it's easy if you do just one thing:

Lead with your core values at all times.

If you've gotten this far into the book, you should have figured this out already: your core values are going to be the lifeblood of *all* aspects of your business. One of the biggest mistakes I see entrepreneurs make is creating a bunch of core values and then never referencing them again. Out of sight, out of mind. Then they're confused about why they have so much turnover or why they can't seem to find the right vendors and partnerships.

I know I'm talking to a really motivated group of people in this book, and I know you all just want to hit the ground running with your business. I get it! But do yourself a favor and slow down. Don't just hire people to fill seats—onboarding people takes time, energy, and money, and you want to be sure that the people you're hiring and working with are truly a match for you and your values. Don't let desperation lead you into mistakes.

Lead with your CORE VALUES AT **ALL TIMES.**

It's never too late to
IMPLEMENT
CORE VALUES
IN YOUR TEAM
and start living by them daily.

You already know you need to be modeling your core values at all times, but when it comes to respecting the potential and significance in everyone, you'll find that it can feel lonely on your climb to "the top," so to speak. Here's what I know, however. If you value each and every person on your way to "the top" (whatever that means for you), you have never been and never will be "alone." In fact, you don't want to make it to "the top" alone. If you do, you're probably a pretty shitty leader.

Owning your own business is great in many ways, but if you're someone who needs constant affirmation and external motivation, this can feel hard. The hard truth is that leadership doesn't come naturally to everyone.

If that is you, that's okay. You can learn this. And the good news is that **it's never too late to implement core values in your team and start living by them daily.** This doesn't have to be painful or cheesy. Take some time by yourself to consider the things you expect and demand of the environment you're creating. That's it. Use my core values as a baseline if you want, but you don't have to.

Your core values have to be real and honest *for you* if you want them to work to help steer your ship.

Write them down. Share them with your team. Hang them up where you and your team can see them daily. Lead by your consistent example.

When I think back on Mr. Enke and what he did for me all those years ago, it wasn't one specific "thing" he did or said. When I was a kid, I thought that being a successful "grown-up" would mean getting a certain job, a certain salary, a certain destination. He showed me that my potential was infinite—a journey with no end.

That's why I'm constantly reading self-help books and books on psychology and self-improvement. I want to challenge myself to think and dream bigger, and I want to be able to provide that same motivation to my team. Not some "we're all in this together" bullshit, but something given to each person, individually.

That's what respecting the potential and significance in each and every person means to me. Seeing them for who they are and for all they are capable of achieving.

Just like Mr. Enke did for me.

5
NEVER COMPROMISE
TRUTH

I WANT TO TAKE YOU BACK to that not-so-great day I told you about in the introduction. Remember that? The day my employee tried to cash the paycheck I'd given them, and I only had $42.86 in my bank account?

That day.

(If you forget the story, go back to the introduction and reread. It's quite the doozy.)

There are a couple details I left out of the introduction that belong in this chapter, where we talk about core values around never compromising truth. I've found that a lot of people *talk* about the importance of telling the truth, being truthful, valuing truth—blah blah blah. But when push comes to shove . . . when they're cornered by their employee, who has been told that their paycheck couldn't be cashed due to insufficient funds . . . well, let's just say they become a bit less hard-core about "never compromising truth."

In fact, they're more than happy to compromise truth if it means saving face.

That's exactly what I did.

Keep in mind, I was young. I was green. I was totally oblivious to the back end of running a business. I didn't understand vendors' terms and conditions, cash flow management, or the seasonal pattern of the industry. In my naivete, I thought that my ability to run my own life, to organize and be responsible with my own finances, was enough.

But that excuse only cuts it so far.

The truth was, I was stubborn. I had that entrepreneurial fire that has served me well, but I hadn't yet learned that in order for me to make it, I was going to have to lean on others for support. I wasn't making time for continuous learning—I was just hustling on hyperspeed.

At the time, I might have said that I would never compromise the truth. I would have believed it, because that seemed like what all good leaders would do.

But when I was approached about the insufficient funds by my employee, I had two options:

1. **I could own up to it.** I could tell my employee that I was so sorry about this, and that I was going to go to the bank and fix it so she could cash the check that afternoon. I could tell her that I appreciated her patience and was so sorry for the inconvenience. I could go to the bank, realize my error, and commit myself right then and there to be more responsible with my business finances.

2. **I could lie.** I could huff and puff about how the bank must have made some sort of error, and I was going to get to the bottom of it. No way I was going to let anyone see the sheer terror in my face or the sweat on my brow on the way out. I could take this mistake to my grave—no one ever needed to know.

You all know which one I chose.

But guess what? It's worse than that. After I'd gone to the bank and *withdrawn from my personal savings to cover my employee paychecks that week*, I went back to my shop and doubled down. I stood by my story that there was some sort of crazy "issue" at the bank, and they were going to resolve it.

Want to know the worst part? My employees believed me. Those lies sat in my stomach like a ton of bricks until . . . well, now. Writing this book. I still look back on that story with dread, even after nineteen years. Because while I'd "figured it out" and saved face, I'd compromised the truth.

And I vowed never to do that again.

THE OH SHIT MENTALITY

One of the most important things you need to hear as a leader, especially in this age of perfectly curated social media posts that are really just smoke and mirrors, is this:

Having an "Oh SHIT!" mentality will absolutely bury you.

Here's what I mean by an "Oh SHIT!" mentality. Let's go back to those days and weeks after my whole "issue at the bank" fiasco. I'd covered up my stupidity all right, but my relief was short lived.

How was I going to replenish the funds from my personal savings account? And more importantly, how the *hell* was I going to shift my business operations so I was making enough money to make payroll every week? And how could I figure out how to do this *yesterday*?!

Mistakes happen. That's given. What's not given is deception. My lie about payroll was the first in a series of dominoes that fell. I had to bust my ass to make more revenue, but I also *couldn't let on to anyone that I had to bust my ass to make more revenue.*

Having an "OH SHIT" MENTALITY WILL ABSOLUTELY **BURY YOU.**

Mistakes happen. THAT'S A GIVEN. WHAT'S NOT GIVEN IS **DECEPTION.**

I was frantic. And worse, I was alone in my worry and panic. Trust me, shit happens. I know that, you know that. But I'd made it a hundred times worse for myself by allowing this mistake to be the thing that set my mindset going forward. I had to get resourceful, which is fine. But I had to get resourceful *all while that gross feeling in the pit of my stomach churned and churned because I'd compromised the truth.* That's an "Oh SHIT!" mentality.

I've seen more than one leader succumb to this mentality. There's only so long you can keep up a frantic pace before you burn out. Want to know what my life looked like while I tried to keep my business afloat and make sure my embarrassing little secret stayed a secret?

- I walked my ass into each and every small business around me with a fresh bouquet of flowers and a stack of business cards to advertise.
- I hosted field trips for kids to come to my shop and see how to run a business. (Ironic, isn't it? They probably knew more about how to run a business than I did at that time.)
- I became a booster and a sponsor for all our local sports events—anything for that low budget advertising.
- I went through my trash—literally. I created "dead bouquets" of flowers for people to give as gag gifts . . . and they were a hit!
- I opened my shop as a free "hot cocoa pit stop" along the town's Christmas parade route just to get people in the door to check out all I had to offer.
- I cut my hair for Locks of Love. Yes, you read that right. I cut my hair. But I didn't do it because I really wanted to. I did it because I knew that the local paper would cover my story, which would in turn give me front-page advertising that I otherwise couldn't afford. In fact, I called the paper to see what day had their highest circulation (Wednesday) and timed my haircut so my article would be featured in that edition. This paper circulated to six surrounding cities—and I delivered to all of them. So I said goodbye to fourteen inches of hair and hello to a front-page newspaper article and an increase in business.

Yeah, it's funny now. And in some ways, I welcomed the fresh start and the renewed energy. Sometimes having an "Oh SHIT!" mentality isn't all bad if it forces you to get resourceful. But I'm a painfully honest person, even now. You know by this point in the book that I practice what I preach. That level of hustle combined with compromising what I knew to be my values was totally unsustainable. And it felt awful!

Don't think that just because you're "older and wiser" you're immune to this. You're not. You will be faced with mistakes and screw-ups, and you will have a choice in how you handle them.

My best advice is to not operate from a place of fear. **Hit the process button before you hit the panic button.**

Yes, doing that at the time would have meant eating some serious crow. Every one of my insecurities as an entrepreneur was at stake.

The honest way isn't always the easier way, but that's business. That's life. You'll have to choose your hard path. I know now that the honest path is always the right one, even if it's hard.

LEADING WITH THE TRUTH

If you've made it this far in the book, you know that as a leader, you really don't have a choice when it comes to your responsibility to the truth. Your employees deserve the truth from you, and so do your customers. And this goes beyond day-to-day operations and even huge, gigantic screw-ups.

It really is about going back to your core values. **Leading with your core values.** Getting to a place where operating from a place of honesty is habitual.

Don't confuse this with being an asshole. Like I said, I'm brutally honest with people, but that doesn't give me a license to be unkind. We all live in glass houses at the end of the day, right?

The best part about leading with truth means that you're going to organically build solid relationships. This isn't hard. For example, back in my flower-shop days, I used to do tons of weddings. I can't tell you how many brides would come to me with hopes of having tulips for their July wedding.

Hit the
PROCESS BUTTON
before you hit the
PANIC BUTTON.

"I love tulips! They're my favorite! I can't get married without them!" If you know anything about flowers, you know that intense heat and tulips do not mix. And July in the Midwest can be brutally hot and humid. Tulips for a July wedding are never going to work out well.

I had a choice—I could simply nod my head, give the customer what she wanted, and live with the fact that she was going to be unhappy. Her problem, right? I'd have already made the sale.

Or I could tell her—kindly, of course—that this decision wasn't in her best interest. I could be totally honest and say that I love tulips too, and they're beautiful in the spring. But in the summer, she'd be so much happier with other flowers that would provide the same look and feel.

Think about what this did. First, and most importantly, it put the happiness of the customer first, before my sale. Second, it showed my expertise—when it came to flowers, I knew what I was talking about. And third, it showed I could be trusted. This meant that while the bride might have been disappointed that she couldn't get her favorite flower on her big day, she also would tell her friends and family that she knew a florist who would never steer them wrong. Those referrals were amazing for my business, so amazing that I continued to do weddings for people eight years after I sold my flower shop—all from word of mouth!

Of course, leading with the truth doesn't start and stop with you. Your teams and partners should share this core value as well. It's holding each other accountable and telling people the hard truth (but with kindness), even when it feels awkward and hard.

You don't do it because it's easy, you do it because it's right.

The good news is that in the age of social media, this type of authenticity will serve you well. People love connecting with other people who are willing to be vulnerable and honest with them. They love knowing that when there are a billion different vendors and products and opinions, they can count on you to be honest and forthcoming—that you're not going to sell them on a bunch of bullshit they don't need.

A word of warning to all you social media #bossbabes and the like: people's BS detectors are fine-tuned nowadays. They can smell dishonesty from a mile away. What I remind the people I coach is that **your reputation is something you painstakingly build for a long time, but it only takes a few moments to tear it apart.**

YOU DON'T DO IT BECAUSE IT'S EASY, you do it because IT'S RIGHT.

YOU WANT TO LEAD WITH YOUR VALUES but also with the HUMANITY OF THE PEOPLE YOU'RE EMPLOYING AND SERVING.

I don't say this to scare you. (Well, no, maybe I do.) I say it because if you lead with honesty, you avoid this fate. It's as simple (and sometimes as hard) as leading with the truth.

THE ART OF THE COMPROMISE

Sometimes the "truth" in your business isn't going to be black or white, right or wrong. We know that there can be gray areas around the best way to do things. Your truth might not always be "the" truth, and the same goes for your team.

That's why my core value around the truth includes the word **compromise**. Yes, there will be times when you have to compromise. A good leader isn't so rigid and self-righteous that it's their way or the highway all the time. But there will also be times where you won't and can't compromise.

The way I see it, there's a subtle art to compromising, and it starts with you, the leader, getting honest about what you're willing to compromise on and what you're not. For me, I don't compromise on quality. Never, ever. But I'm definitely willing to compromise on process, especially if it's because a vendor or team member that I have a great relationship with has an amazing idea that I never thought of before.

I mentioned in chapter 2 that I am never afraid to tell someone on my team that their work is not their best work, but that doesn't mean I call out every little thing. Sometimes being too honest can create a toxic work environment too. Not every issue needs to be code-red levels of brutal honesty.

So where's that fine line? I don't know. You have to figure that out, as the leader. What I tell people I coach is this:

You want to lead with your values, but also with the humanity of the people you're employing and serving.

This is where the whole idea of "process before panic" really comes into play. If, when the shit hits the fan, you take a moment to simply acknowledge your humanity and the humanity of others, you have a chance to be truthful in a way that builds trust, not panic.

Relationships first, remember?

I could have done this all those years ago at the flower shop. I could have explained to my team that I'd screwed up, that I was relying on them to help me not do it again. But at that moment, I was so caught up in my own ego that I didn't see that I wouldn't have lost respect. I would have *gained* it by leading with the truth.

This can feel scary as a leader, but after many years as an entrepreneur, I know it's not. It's really as simple as going back to the Golden Rule. But finding the right balance between truth and humanity is the key.

PROCESS BEFORE PANIC, DAILY

Process before panic is really a mindset more than anything else. "Mindset" is another one of those woo-woo words that everyone and their mother throws out on social media nowadays, but in this case it's true. Getting out of an "Oh SHIT!" mindset and into a more thoughtful one where you're focused on the long game is an essential part of running a business, but also of being a good leader.

Here's what this looks like as a daily practice for me:

- **Direct, clear, and kind communication.** Someone's not pulling their fair share of the weight on my team? I address it directly and quickly. Customer's asking something of me that's outside my comfort zone? I say no firmly, kindly, and clearly. Vendor's disappointing me with their recent shipments? I have a candid conversation about my expectations and how they are not being met.

- **Honesty.** We're going to talk a lot more about honesty in the next chapter, but for now it should be pretty obvious that I'm never willing to spare someone's feelings if it means I'm compromising my values or integrity. My honesty is one of my most important qualities to me as a leader, but that doesn't mean I'm constantly making people feel like shit. If you take nothing else from this chapter, take this: **honesty is the best policy, but an even better policy is to wrap your honesty in kindness. Relationships first.**
- **Lead with wanting the best for your business.** It can be so easy to get caught up in the project, the sale, the moment. But for me, that just keeps you stuck spinning the same wheels, over and over. When I make decisions on a daily basis, even small ones, I'm always leading with what is best for my company and my business as a whole. My team, my vendors, my customers, and my ultimate vision for what I want.
- **Surround yourself with the right people.** You know what they say—don't dish it out if you can't take it. The last thing you want as an entrepreneur and leader is to surround yourself with a bunch of people who are going to tell you only what you want to hear. The "no pandering, no bullshit" rule that I have applies to my team too. The nice thing about owning your own company is that you are able to carefully vet the people you bring into the fold. Make sure you don't bring in a bunch of yes-people who won't challenge you or hold you accountable.

Much of this mindset practice really goes hand in hand with being a good business person. Despite the ups and downs of every day, you want to stay focused on the big picture. Always. Does this mean you might have fewer sales sometimes? Yes. Does it mean you might have to pull back on a project because you know the end product is not going to meet your and your customers' expectations? Also yes.

Does this mean you're going to have to suck it up and own it when you screw up? Absolutely yes. The good news is that the more you practice these skills, the easier it becomes.

I speak from experience so trust me on this one.

HINDSIGHT IS 20/20

It's easy to look back on our mistakes and kick ourselves for not doing what was obviously the right thing at the time. God knows I *still* cringe thinking back to that day in the bank, staring at $42.86 in my account.

The nice thing about being nearly twenty years past that time of my life is that I have the benefit of hindsight. It was through that experience that I realized never compromising truth needed to be one of my core values from that day forward.

When I work with people in their businesses, they always ask me what I wish I'd known starting out. I'm a firm believer that there's nothing better than learning from your own mistakes, but until then, here you go:

- **Get to the root of the need.** When I think back to that moment in the bank and employees who had checks they couldn't cash, my first impulse was to fix the problem, clear the checks, and move on. Looking back, I know I was only putting lipstick on a pig, so to speak. The root of the issue was that I was missing some fundamental business knowledge. I needed to fix that—stat—if I wanted to succeed long term, so I began to educate myself more and more.
- **Realize that you, your team, and your customers deserve more.** I was in such an "Oh SHIT!" mentality at that moment that I was leading with the intention of saving face. The truth was, my team deserved better of me, their leader. And you know what? *I* deserved better of me. I wish that I would have recognized that in that moment and in the scramble that was to come as I tried to fix my mess.
- **Surround yourself with the right people.** Yes, I realize I just said this in the previous section, but it's true. I wish I would have intentionally surrounded myself with other entrepreneurs, especially when I was first starting out. They might have saved me from my own stupidity!

- **Seek truth and meaning over emotional gratification.** This is tough. When I was first starting out, I was terrified of being wrong or hurting people's feelings. Now I know that operating from a place of fear as a leader is no way to run a business. It will bite you in the ass in all sorts of ways, some of which you might not be able to recover from.

The bottom line is that while compromise is part of the deal when it comes to relationships, you need to be secure in exactly who you are and what you value when you choose to lead a team. Ayn Rand might have said it best:

"There can be no compromise on basic principles, moral issues, matters of truth or rational conviction."

And there it is. You have to **know your truth first** if you want to be the kind of leader who finds not just financial success, but personal and professional success as well.

> YOU NEED TO BE **SECURE** IN **WHO YOU ARE** and **what you value** WHEN YOU CHOOSE TO LEAD A TEAM.

6
ACT WITH HONESTY AND INTEGRITY

YOU MIGHT BE THINKING that after that $42.86 story, I'd be done talking about telling the truth.

Not a chance.

Truth—telling it, living it, and knowing it for yourself—is important. But that value doesn't begin and end with one-off mess-ups or forgiving yourself and others for their newbie mistakes. It expands far bigger into how you conduct yourself as a leader when things completely outside your control happen too.

Things you can't easily fix. Things that will require you to be vulnerable and scared. Things that will threaten all you've worked so hard to achieve. Things that leave you with no clear path to move forward.

And trust me, those situations will come up for you often. No matter how much you plan, no matter how much you pray. That's life.

This is where acting with honesty and integrity comes in. I think of this as going beyond situational moments in time that can be fixed and forgotten.

Just think about the word **integrity** and see what I mean. Integrity implies a strong moral character, someone who leads with principles.

Who in your life do you see as having integrity?

When I think of the people in my life who have the most integrity, they aren't always the most successful business people. Their integrity has nothing to do with how much money they make or how many fancy things they buy.

Their integrity is a direct reflection of who they are. I don't just trust them to tell me the truth, I know in my heart that they lead their lives with truth. Even when it's hard.

I respect the hell out of them for it. *That's* integrity.

Honesty and integrity are two sides of the same coin for me. **Think of this core value as the foundation of the business you've built.** It's more than telling the truth; it's establishing a foundation that will not be compromised for the lifetime of your business. That foundation will set the tone for everything, from your day-to-day interactions with your customers and teams to the way you steer your ship when the shit hits the fan.

Especially when major shit hits the fan.

THEIR INTEGRITY IS A DIRECT REFLECTION OF WHO THEY ARE.

I don't just trust them to tell me the truth, I KNOW IN MY HEART THAT **THEY LEAD THEIR LIVES WITH TRUTH.** *Even when it's hard.*

WHEN THINGS ARE OUT OF YOUR CONTROL

In September of 2020, I launched my newest business, The Paper & Plan Co. Let's just say that I was a lot smarter and more prepared than I was when I was twenty and ran the flower shop. Everything, from the products I was selling to the presentation of my new business, was my very, very best work.

Because I'd built so many solid relationships on social media (more on this later), my prelaunch mainly happened there. I did Instagram Lives, posted teasers for my new products, and shared behind-the-scenes pictures of what I was up to. I built excitement carefully and intentionally, but also very genuinely. "Excited" doesn't come close to describing how I felt when I finally opened my business up for preorders.

The presales were instant and overwhelming. Even though I had planned for exactly that outcome, I still could hardly believe how well received that launch was. I was set and confirmed to receive my 2021 planners in mid-October, ready to have them all shipped out by early November and enjoy a great holiday season celebrating all that hard work.

Did I mention this was September **2020**? You know, the year COVID-19 brought the world to a standstill?

In early October, I reached out to the printer to confirm receipt of the planners. "All set for a mid-October delivery, right?" I asked.

"Well . . ." the printer said timidly. "There are some issues in Canada. The pandemic has backed everything up."

I took a deep breath. "Okay," I said. "How much of a delay are we looking at?"

"End of October," they guessed. "Should be better by then."

I had a sinking feeling in my stomach. I'd promised my customers they would receive their preordered planners by early-November. This was cutting it way too close for my comfort.

The end of October rolled around, and still no planners. My heart raced every time I called the printer. "Please," I said. "I need to know what I'm dealing with here. *Where* are my planners?"

"They're stuck in Canada, Emily. I'm sorry, but there's nothing we can do about it. Everything is backed up. They just don't have the manpower to get through all of them and get them shipped." The first of November came and went with no planners. I was so beside myself that I actually booked a flight to Canada, planning to rent a U-Haul so I could rescue the planners and drive as many of them as I could from Canada back to Missouri so I could get them shipped out on time. I canceled only when I found out that there was no way of knowing which containers would be mine—and even if I knew *that*, they still wouldn't release them to me anyway.

Then, the middle of November came. Still no planners.

You know me and my philosophy well enough by now to know that this situation was the perfect storm. My absolute biggest nightmare.

I knew I had to tell the truth to my customers, so that's exactly what I did. During those agonizing weeks, I was spending day and night sending emails to my customers, providing updates as best I could. I responded to inquiries quickly; I apologized profusely.

But the truth was only going to get me so far. My entire brand and reputation were on the line, and I knew it.

On December 8—*December* 8—I finally received the planners. As you can probably imagine, from the second those boxes appeared, it was all hands on deck. We wrapped and shipped those planners in record time, just grateful to be able to make it before the end of the year.

Phew, I thought as those final shipments went out in the nick of time. *We made it.*

Not so fast.

The domino effect of the pandemic crisis reached the post office too. Remember that?

Let's just say I was working customer service 24/7 at that point. I knew what was happening was beyond my control and not my "fault." But what good was that when I knew I was disappointing my customers?

Business is personal, remember?

I was very open and transparent about what was going on.

And you know what I discovered? Of the thousands of planners I presold, I can count on one hand the number of people who were genuinely angry about the delay. For the most part, when I sent out emails with my apologies, I got responses that looked like this:

Thank you so much for letting me know. I'm disappointed, but I know this situation is beyond your control. I appreciate you keeping me posted. Have a great holiday!

I attribute this gracious reaction to my honesty in the situation, but also to **the integrity of my brand that I'd worked so hard to create**. People knew me and trusted that I was doing absolutely everything in my power to meet their expectations. Yes, I'd fallen short, but I'd owned it and was doing everything in my power to make it right.

The relationships I'd built ended up saving me and my business. I'd shown honesty and integrity, which I've discovered are rare things in this messed-up world we live in.

CUSTOMER SERVICE, WITH HONESTY AND INTEGRITY

The 2020 planner launch debacle is in the rearview mirror now, thank God. But when I look back on that crisis, I realize that it was customer service that really saved my entire brand and business. It will be the same for you.

Entrepreneurs and leaders in general have a tendency to overthink what customer service really means. Their egos are so fragile that the thought of acting with honesty and integrity terrifies them. My advice: don't overthink it. **Simply treat your customers the way you would want to be treated in that situation.** My customer service wasn't complicated; it was genuine and real.

I let people know I was just as frustrated as they were.

I made sure my customers knew I appreciated every single sale.

SIMPLY TREAT YOUR CUSTOMERS THE WAY YOU WOULD WANT TO BE TREATED IN THAT SITUATION.

I acknowledged and recognized I was impacting their holiday seasons and their lives.

I kept my heart open to hearing their disappointment. I saw the humanity in each and every person I was connecting with.

Again, I was overwhelmingly met with gratitude and understanding, despite the fact that I could not fix the problem. We've been so conditioned to think that everyone's out to scam us that I think people were disarmed and genuinely grateful that I was meeting them where they were and taking responsibility.

And that is what so many leaders miss. You don't need to give yourself a heart attack trying to fix problems and avoid confrontation that might make you look bad. Providing customer service that is centered on the humanity of the person is often enough.

HONESTY AND INTEGRITY ON SOCIAL MEDIA

I obviously can't have a chapter about honesty and integrity and not talk about social media. You and I both see it all the time: people showing off their perfectly curated lives and using all the nonsense hashtags like #blessed #sixfigures #winner. These people are putting a highlight reel out there that is meant to show you exactly what they want you to see.

And we're *on* to that bullshit.

The truth is that all the smoke-and-mirrors BS is causing people to lose trust in social media. How could they not? You've got nineteen-year-old life coaches out there pretending they have figured out the world (give me a break), and entrepreneurs who are showing off a "reality" that anyone with Google can figure out is not real.

For some people, this is so off-putting that they want to avoid social media altogether. I hear it from people all the time—they just don't have any interest in being there if it's all a bunch of fluff and garbage.

For me, it's obvious that **there is a huge opportunity in all the noise of social media—an opportunity for people who want to be honest and build genuine, long-lasting relationships**. For people who are willing to be vulnerable and bold enough to put their passion and heart out there for the world to see. Not just the good stuff, but the bad stuff too. The *real* stuff.

People's distrust in social media is your opportunity to present yourself as the exception to all the crap out there. You will naturally rise to the top if you're leading with honesty and integrity.

That's easy for you to say, I can hear people saying. *You already have your profile and brand established. But I'm just starting out. There's so much competition, it's paralyzing.*

I understand the hesitation. There *is* a ton of perceived competition these days, in every space imaginable. I can only respond with what has worked for me, and it's this: I don't pay attention to the competition. I don't watch other people of influence and entrepreneurs, endlessly comparing them to me. I just do what is right for me, my brand, and my team.

Do I like, follow, and learn from other entrepreneurs? Of course. I watch for what they do well and get inspired and excited by their successes. But if your eyes are always on the competition, worried about what they're doing and how it compares to what you do, then you're going to be wasting a lot of time and energy in the long run.

DON'T FEED THE TROLLS

I'm always going to encourage people to be their authentic selves and use social media to establish their brands with honesty and integrity, but I'm never going to tell you that it's quick or easy. As you already know, building these trusted relationships takes time.

And yes, you'll also have to deal with trolls.

Before I tell you my simple way of dealing with trolls on the internet, I want to acknowledge what *not* to do. It can be so tempting to delete comments that are not exactly favorable. I see people and brands doing this all the time. They are trying to make it so their social profiles are filled with enthusiasm, falsely assuming that 100 percent positivity is a good marketing tool for their product and brand.

But that's not honest, is it? To me, it's a missed opportunity to establish trusting relationships. When I see how brands handle complaints and issues on their social media sites, I get a true sense of what they are all about. Oftentimes, I appreciate their honesty and transparency so much that I'm willing to take a chance on that product if I haven't before. At the very least, I know that if I reach out to them, I won't get ghosted or deleted, and that means something to me.

Look, trolls happen. My advice: **never feed the trolls**. Don't engage, and don't waste your time or energy with their negativity.

It's rare, but when I get a trollish comment on my social media, I respond with the same two letters: "OK."

Sarcastic comment? "OK."

Not into my dogs? "OK."

Have something to say about the wallpaper in the background of my picture? "OK."

I don't delete, but I don't waste energy. All the trolls want is for you to engage them, and a simple "OK" sends them scrambling off to find someone else to bother.

All that time and energy I *don't* waste on trolls goes directly to my real customers, my VIPs. I engage with them, show my sincere gratitude, and make real connections. I share my real life, even when it's imperfect and messy—and people are hungry for that kind of authenticity. I would never relinquish control of my social media to an assistant—why would I?

Relationships first. *Real* relationships first.

HONESTY AND INTEGRITY ARE CONTAGIOUS

I know I said this before, but I find it sad that honesty and integrity aren't a given in our culture. Looking back at handling the crises of my 2020 The

Paper & Plan Co launch, it's clear that had I done anything other than be truthful, apologetic, and empathetic with my customers, I would have had ten times the heartache and stress.

It's really not that hard, is it?

Remember when you were a kid, and how it felt to lie to your teacher about why you were missing your homework assignment? Or to your parents about whose house you were going to for the night when you were in high school? That feeling just sits in the pit of your stomach, causing the stress to compound. Even if you got away with the lie, you might have felt okay for a moment, but you ultimately felt pretty shitty about yourself.

Well, you're a grown-up now, and you aren't just starting a business. You're showing others your moral character, each and every day. This isn't mind-blowingly hard work. **Who you are and what you stand for should be obvious to everyone you come into contact with—not just with your words, but with your actions too.**

Of course, sales are important. Making money is important. I'm not saying you should stand so firmly in some sort of moral self-righteousness that you make everything about your perfect moral character and don't give a thought to paying the bills.

What I'm saying is that **when you start and lead with being grounded in who you are and what you stand for, the sales will naturally come.** You won't be chasing them down like some slimy used car salesman. Your honesty and integrity will draw people to you organically.

The best part is that leading in this way is infectious. Your teams will watch you in action, see you own mistakes with dignity, and emulate you. Your customers will know that they can trust you with their hard-earned money and time, and give you grace if (and when) things out of your control happen. You won't have to teach people to be honest and act with integrity; they'll just do it.

Well, mostly. There are always going to be people for whom your example, your best efforts, and your honesty and integrity aren't enough. Those people are going to give you a run for your money.

I'm not going to lie—those times are not fun. Letting go of those toxic people and partnerships can be hard and make you doubt yourself.

When you start and lead with **BEING GROUNDED IN WHO YOU ARE** AND **WHAT YOU STAND FOR** *the sales will naturally come.*

One book I like to recommend to people is *The Four Agreements*, by Don Miguel Ruiz. His philosophy helps put into perspective that you can really only control you—how you act, how you respond, how you judge. Honesty is not always the easiest path, and feelings do get hurt from time to time. It can feel hard to make yourself vulnerable to that.

But you must. You're not going to please everyone, and you're going to have to learn to live with other people's disappointments in you sometimes.

That sort of strength will also be infectious. It will help your teams and everyone you work with be more resilient as you weather the ups and downs of the entrepreneur's life. You'll sleep better, have a clearer head for decision making, and be able to really enjoy your success, because you didn't compromise yourself in order to achieve it.

HONESTY, INTEGRITY, AND EVERYDAY CUSTOMER SERVICE

Like it or not, as a business owner you are in the business of customer service. No matter what you're creating, offering, or selling, the customer's experience should be what guides you each and every day.

Does that mean that the customer is always right? Probably not. I don't love that old adage because it doesn't allow for any nuance or interpretation. If someone who's purchased one of my planners reviews it with one star and says something like, "I could get a planner that does the same thing from Target for five bucks," she's not *wrong*, not really. She's right that she could get a planner for cheaper. But she was wrong in purchasing a planner from me, not because my product isn't good, but because she doesn't value the quality I've provided.

And that's fine. Remember when we talked about **making it your best work**? I never said that your best work would be the perfect product for everyone. If someone wants to buy a cheaper planner that doesn't include all the "extras" I provide, that's totally okay by me. I'm going to remain focused on the customers who *do* value my product.

You will do the same balancing act for the lifetime of your business—finding the happy medium between staying true to your core values while also being okay dealing with criticism and complaints.

All this is to say that customer service is part of the deal. Not just when the shit hits the fan, but every single day. I prefer to think of customer service as customer *care*. I lead by **providing care for their experience, from the moment they are made aware of my brand to the experience they have using my products**. I take this mentality into designing my products, choosing my vendors and team, and responding to customer ideas and feedback.

Providing outstanding customer care is a daily practice. Here are some ways I work with others to get them into the practice of providing excellent customer care:

- **Humanize your brand.** People really underestimate the power of sharing your brand's story. It doesn't have to be on social media (though that's such an easy place to start). Take your customers behind the scenes; show them the care you put into your products and decisions. This doesn't mean oversharing. You can have as many boundaries as you're comfortable with. But in this day and age, when we can buy all sorts of stuff on Amazon for cheap, make you and your brand stand out by being a real live human who cares about making a quality product for their customers.
- **Own your mistakes.** I'm living proof that owning your mistakes— even when it sucks—is the way to go. Don't waste time trying to be perfect. You won't be. Instead, focus on being honest, not shifting blame, and being empathetic to your customer's experience.

- **Don't sell all the damn time.** You do not need to make every customer interaction about making a sale. Just communicate for the sake of creating relationships. Entrepreneurs tend to overthink their social media posts, trying to monetize each and every one. It's a huge turnoff to your customers and doesn't do anything to create a loyal fanbase.
- **Don't ignore your customers and audience.** Engage with your customers. Think of them as your VIPs and the lifeblood of your business, because *they are*. This goes beyond social media and into every interaction you have. It's hard to overstate how powerful this type of customer care is. It will establish your authority and integrity with people who will want to come back to you time and again for your expertise.

Again, this isn't hard—it goes back to the Golden Rule. It's a shame that we are so cynical and distrustful of people's intentions nowadays; we all have our stories of being burned, but the good news is that you as a leader and business owner have the opportunity to be part of changing that, simply by acting with honesty and integrity.

7

PROMOTE
A CULTURE OF INNOVATION AND CONTINUOUS
IMPROVEMENT

"At my company, we value innovation."

"Here, we want to continuously improve ourselves and our products."

"Part of what gets me super excited about my business is being inspired to always be better, every single day."

On paper, all this sounds great. These are the types of companies we all want to work for, right? Ones that are always looking to the future, reaching for the stars?

But if you ask me, statements like these can be dangerously woo-woo, froufrou, "You can do it" nonsense if you're not careful. Meaningless platitudes don't do jack for your business if you don't put them into real, actual practice.

If you are the type of business owner who really, truly believes in innovation and continuous improvement as central to your core values, this chapter is for you.

No fluff.

Action.

DISRUPT YOUR INDUSTRY

Chances are your big, awesome, amazing idea has been done before. At the very least, it's a spin-off of something that has been done before. That's okay. Many people mistakenly think that for a product to be innovative, it needs to be brand new—something no one has ever heard of before.

Sure, that can be innovation. But if you ask me, **innovation is more than just the product you're delivering.** It's the way that you deliver it. It's the way that you continuously improve it. It's the way that you, as the business owner, look at your product and think about how it can be helpful to other people—and then *even more* helpful to *even more* people beyond that.

In other words, **being an innovator means being a disrupter to your industry.** You see a problem and you solve it. Maybe the product is innovative by itself, or maybe it's the way you deliver that product. Maybe your innovation is the way you provide customer service. Maybe it's the ordering experience. Maybe it's the style with which you market your products.

INNOVATION
IS **MORE** THAN
just the product you're delivering.

Innovation is everywhere. Take the company Zappos, for example. An online store is hardly a brand-new concept, but when people shop at Zappos, they aren't shopping for a particularly innovative *product*. They're shopping there because Zappos disrupted the industry with their amazing shipping and return policy. Their success shows just how far-reaching the concept of innovation can be.

Or take my company, The Paper & Plan Co. I make planners. Calendars and planning are hardly new, innovative ideas. But I knew when I started that I had a product that was different, that could disrupt the industry.

How did I do that? Simple. I took the planner that I'd been using and thought, *You know what? This planner would be so much better if it had a more durable cover, a place to hold my Top Five Priorities. And you know what else? If it had places for me to jot down my fitness and meal plan. Oh, and you know what would make it even better? Time blocks and beautiful, elegant packaging.* I could innovate the experience for people. I could make a planner that people would really, actually use and appreciate. I could make a planner that would make a great gift.

Don't get me wrong—you can go to any Dollar Store and get a cheap planner for a buck or less. (See chapter 2 for a refresher on my core values around making what I sell my best work.) My innovation is always centered on providing excellent customer service and a great product.

Some business owners will disrupt their industry by making something more affordable for the end user. Others will disrupt their industry by making a product no one has ever heard of before. Maybe they'll innovate around production or sales. The possibilities are endless.

And the best part about all this innovating? It doesn't stop. Your company isn't just about you, what works for you, and what feels innovative to you.

We've already talked about how a big part of the work of being a business owner is listening to your customers. **Relationships first, right?** Often, creating a culture around innovation is as simple as listening to your end customers and taking their feedback to heart.

We'll talk about this more later in the chapter, but here's a simple example of how this works. I'm not an early riser, and my day starts around 8:00 a.m. When my planners first came out, I started each day in the planner at 6:00 a.m. Seemed logical and early enough to me.

Then I got feedback from my customers. "I love this planner, but I start my day at 4:00 a.m. It would be awesome if the daily pages started at four."

With one quick design change, my product became more beneficial to my end customer. And now I'm one of the only planners on the market that starts at 4:00 a.m.

That's innovation.

A CULTURE OF INNOVATION

Business owners are innovating constantly, even if it's just researching the industry, asking for feedback, or simply brainstorming with their team.

We already know that when people think of innovation, they think of something new, like a process or a service. These days, when we think of a new process or service, we think of tech. Technology can definitely be a form of innovation, but that's not necessarily always the case. In his book *Strategic Management*, Frank Rothaermel claims that there are four types of innovation in business:

1. **Incremental.** This is the innovation that happens slowly and continually, based on knowledge you get through your existing markets and data. For example, you have a product, you receive feedback on that product, and you make a change based on that feedback. That's incremental innovation.
2. **Radical.** This is the innovation that happens because your company is trying to target a new market or utilize a new technology. For example, you offer a certain product, but you know that you will have to change your shipping strategies in order to sell that product overseas. Taking a chance on this new model in a new market would be radical innovation.
3. **Architectural.** This is the innovation that happens when you take your product and make it more accessible and/or valuable to the end user. For example, say you have a company that makes sunscreen. You look at your competition and realize that their product offers five hours of protection. You rework your product to offer six hours of protection. That is architectural innovation.

4. **Disruptive.** This is the innovation that happens when you create a product that disrupts and changes the market with the help of new "technology." For example, look at how the digital camera revolutionized how we take, print, and share photos. We are saturated with these sorts of disruptive innovations all the time, which is both a good and bad thing!

I get it—all this potential for innovation can be really overwhelming. *My team and I have to be thinking about innovation like this every single day?* In a word, yes. But it's often as simple as just being open to feedback. When you create a culture and habit around listening, interacting, and creating open lines of communication between you, your customers, and your teams, knowing when and how to innovate becomes much simpler.

Relationships first.

Leaders aren't doing this enough. They talk the talk of innovation from their platforms, but when it comes to actually listening to criticism from their customers and teams, their egos get in the way.

There is a lot of excuse-making around being busy. *I'm too busy to be thinking about innovation today—maybe next quarter.* Any productivity book out there will tell you that "busy" does not equal productive. In fact, the busier you are, the more of a red flag it is. **You should never be too busy to take in feedback and use it to make the experience for your customers and your teams better.**

I often tell people I work with that innovation is meant not to complicate things, but to simplify them. Don't get me wrong—of course you will be stressed out and busy at times! I'm not saying you will never have days or even weeks where you have to put everything on hold to handle a crisis of some kind. That's business (and life!). What I'm saying is that you should not be leading from a place of busy-ness and constant "productivity" all the time.

My suggestion to always-busy entrepreneurs who don't have time for innovation is pretty simple. If you get overwhelmed—and you will—put it all down on paper. Need help? Check out the Eisenhower Matrix for Innovation Prioritization. This is what I use when I'm in need of a "reset" to make sure I'm continuing to live by this particular core value.

1. URGENT *and* IMPORTANT	2. NOT URGENT *but* IMPORTANT
3. URGENT *but* NOT IMPORTANT	4. NOT URGENT *and* NOT IMPORTANT

You should never be
TOO BUSY TO TAKE IN FEEDBACK
AND USE IT TO MAKE THE EXPERIENCE
FOR YOUR CUSTOMERS AND TEAMS
BETTER.

Look, I get it. Your business is your baby. You know what's right for it, and you want to give it *everything you've got* to make it successful. **Creating a culture of innovation is really about making sure you aren't so blinded by love of what you've created that you miss glaring issues and/or opportunities for improvement.**

You know what they say about the devil being in the details? Being open to feedback and willing to implement ways to make your product and business even greater is a way to stay ahead of those details and the competition.

CONSISTENT INNOVATION

The bottom line is that as entrepreneurs and business owners, we make innovation a lot harder and scarier than it needs to be. People waste tons of time and money on conferences and campaigns, all in the name of "innovation," when they really don't have to. Like I've already said, innovation doesn't have to involve a huge launch or shift in the way you do things.

Here's how we create a culture of innovation at my companies. Buckle up, everyone.

We have a standing weekly meeting. After we go through the normal business stuff, we go around the room, and everyone voices an idea or a concept to consider that might improve the business.

That's it.

Everyone is required to think of something that might improve the company in some way, and then they say that idea to the team.

Then we take those ideas for innovation and put a plan in place to implement them.

Mind-blowing, right?

Now, don't get me wrong. Is every idea I hear a good one? No. There have been plenty of times when I hear an idea and say, "Yeah . . . not gonna happen." We've had plenty of laughs, debates, and brainstorming sessions as a result of this very simple addition to our weekly meetings.

CREATING A CULTURE OF INNOVATION is really about making sure you aren't so **BLINDED BY LOVE** OF WHAT YOU'VE CREATED **THAT YOU MISS** GLARING ISSUES AND/OR OPPORTUNITIES **FOR IMPROVEMENT**

And again, this is where that **relationships-first mentality** is going to make all the difference. None of these brainstorming sessions around innovation work if you haven't created bonds with the people on your team and showed that you value and respect them. For your team to be vulnerable and offer up their ideas openly, they need to trust you. There's no getting around it. If you try to introduce this practice to your team, just know that the first couple weeks can be as awkward as a middle-school dance—suddenly, everyone will be shy. Simply listen to them, ask why they feel there is a need for that idea/product, and ask how it can improve the overall customer experience or product offering. Then, as the weeks begin to pass, you will see there is a growing sense of excitement in sharing. Now, instead of one new idea, they come with two, three, or four.

Relationships first.

Once you have created those solid, honest relationships, and once you have learned to put your own ego aside and really listen to the ideas of the people in your circle, that's when the simplest and most effective innovation happens.

Here's an example: After The Paper & Plan Co was off the ground and running, I remember having this weekly meeting with my sister Sarah (she's my COO) and some other team members. Sarah said, "You know what we should think about adding? A notepad that will include information for the babysitter. You know, if you go out on a date night and you want to have all the emergency contact information in one spot for whoever is watching the kids?"

I didn't know. I don't have kids. But I also didn't need to be a parent myself to know that my sister's idea was brilliant. We included the "babysitter's pad" in our offerings ASAP, and customers still comment on how helpful it is. See what I mean here? **Continuous innovation starts with creating a great work culture.** Once you have that in place, your mind will be open to all the ways your business can grow.

CONTINUOUS INNOVATION starts with creating a GREAT WORK CULTURE.

CONTINUOUS IMPROVEMENT

We've already talked about how my core values center on continuous improvement. The way I see it, innovation and improvement go hand in hand.

Aside from all the things you're doing to help yourself become a better entrepreneur and leader in general, continuous improvement also means taking a bird's-eye view of your business from time to time, looking for opportunities to learn and grow.

I'm not just talking about obvious things, like looking at your competition and making sure your product and customer experience are better than theirs. If I spent all my continuous-improvement time just looking at other planner companies, I would simply be re-creating what other people are doing—that's the exact opposite of what I want to do. That kind of continuous improvement will only take you so far. And if you're not careful, making your "continuous improvement" revolve around what everyone else is doing could turn you into just another copycat. You will always be years behind.

What I tell people is to think beyond their business and into their brand, their style, and what really inspires them as individuals.

For me, this means that I follow, interact with, and am inspired by food, travel, and design pages on social media. Those types of businesses are related to what I do, when you think about it. I'm not looking at their products or offerings as much as I'm looking at how they brand themselves, their color palettes, and even the moods they create with their aesthetic. I just want to get a vibe from them; then I let the inspiration take flight.

For example, I once saw an image on a food blog that totally caught my eye. It was a closeup of a blueberry.

Yes, you read that right. A closeup of a *blueberry*.

Before you think I'm crazy, hear me out.

This was such a gorgeous photo. The velvet-like texture, the color, the shadowing . . . everything was just so beautiful to me. I thought to myself, *This! This is the aesthetic and feel I want for one of my notebooks!* For me, this type of inspiration happens all the time, and often comes from people outside my industry. Maybe it's because when you remove comparisons and competition, you can keep your mind open to possibility.

I've said it before and I'll say it again: you really can't afford *not* to spend time on innovation and improvement. It's how you and your teams will grow, thrive, and create a sustainable business. But the truth is we live in a culture that glorifies being "busy." It's up to you as an entrepreneur and business leader to create a new mindset that values stepping back and taking time for innovation and continuous improvement.

Here are a couple ways I encourage leaders to do this for themselves and their teams:

- **Implement Dungeon Days.** Take a hard look at your schedule and carve out one day a week where you will not take any meetings, phone conferences, etc. Those days are for taking care of loose ends, following up on items that have fallen through the cracks, and giving yourself some space for innovation and improvement. Think of Dungeon Days as your working vacation to catch up. Don't allow any distractions on this day. You can make your Dungeon Day the same day every week or change it up weekly. Once you get into the habit of implementing Dungeon Days and seeing how much they benefit you, you'll become very protective of them!
- **Welcome boredom.** People nowadays are afraid to be bored. We are surrounded by so many distractions that we literally never have a moment where we don't have anything to "do." (And if we do, we make ourselves feel guilty about it!) I always suggest that people welcome that feeling of being bored. It's during those times that your mind can wander and you can really take time to invite inspiration.
- **Encourage breaks and changes in scenery.** If you are the type of leader who prefers to keep their employees parked behind their desks all day, you should rethink that. Allowing your team to move around the office, work from home one day a week, or go outside for a walk while on a call can be just what is needed to spark their innovation and creativity. Good leaders break the cycle of the mundane nine-to-five jobs and encourage their employees to recharge and get reinspired.

ENJOY THE PROCESS

The good news is that sometimes these efforts to innovate and improve your business are going to be home runs.

The bad news is that sometimes... they're not.

When things fail in your business (and they will, as we know), you have two options:
1. Cower, hide, blame, and swear to never leave the comfort of your bed ever again.
2. Take a breath, step back, and assess where you went wrong and how to do better next time. And as you know, I've been there. I've made mistakes, and plenty of them. You already know to own those mistakes and learn from them, but how do you do that, exactly?

Well, if you ever find any of your efforts to innovate and improve your business to be colossal failures, chances are there are multiple issues involved. Maybe your branding or marketing was off. Maybe you did or did not do something that you should have in hindsight. Maybe you did everything right, but your expectations were off. Maybe you simply weren't consistent enough.

More than likely, it's a combination of a lot of things.

Instead of letting failures crush you, though, you have an opportunity to ask yourself if the effort can be saved.

Yes, that means going back to the drawing board. Did you do everything in your power that you possibly could have to implement this new plan? The answer is probably no. This doesn't make you a bad person, entrepreneur, or business owner.

> Trying again isn't terrible.
> Chalking up a loss isn't terrible.
> Going back to the drawing board isn't terrible.
> *Failing isn't terrible.*

TRYING AGAIN
isn't terrible.
CHALKING UP A LOSS
isn't terrible.
GOING BACK TO THE DRAWING BOARD
isn't terrible.
Failing isn't terrible.

What *is* terrible is when entrepreneurs have such huge egos, along with ego-led expectations, and mix those with their failure to properly forecast. They set themselves up for frustration and failure. In my eyes, no matter how much money they make, if they're so caught up in the rigidity of what they consider to be perfection that they don't enjoy the process of creating a business... what's the point?

I'm not going to lie—enjoying the process can sound like some of that woo-woo bullshit I hate to hear from people. As someone who is always thinking about the next big thing, sometimes taking a moment to "enjoy the process" is hard for me. As in nearly impossible.

This is why innovation and continuous improvement are part of my core values. Of course I want good outcomes when I'm working on something new. I want success, same as you do! So when I think about this core value for myself, I focus on the fact that **the outcome isn't the only thing that matters**. It's getting into the mindset that being a good business owner and leader means being constantly open to inspiration and improvement.

There are going to be dark and gritty moments, moments where you have to innovate if you want to stay relevant. There are going to be times when you feel too overwhelmed to take time for inspiration.

Think about innovation and improvement as muscles you'll need to grow and flex. The more you practice, the stronger and more flexible you'll be over time. When times get difficult and you have built up the strength to pivot, reimagine, and move forward, you're going to be grateful you persevered.

8
SHOW APPRECIATION AND GRATITUDE

I WAS RAISED BY PARENTS WHO impressed upon me at a very young age the importance of having good manners.

I'm not just talking about writing thank-you notes for my birthday gifts, though that was important. I'm talking about showing genuine, sincere thanks. I have memories of picking up the phone to call Grandma and tell her just how I was going to use my birthday money that year. I also have memories of my parents reminding me to look people in the eye when speaking to them, to thank them not just with my words but with my attention and energy.

This wasn't bullshit. My parents weren't teaching me how to manipulate people to get what I want.

They were teaching me that showing appreciation and gratitude is an essential part of building good relationships.

Relationships first.

When these types of manners are instilled in you at a young age, they stay with you forever. I feel so fortunate that by the time I owned my first business, showing gratitude was not something I needed to learn. It was already part of who I was. (Thanks, Mom and Dad!) But I feel there is always room for improvement.

There's a lot of talk about gratitude nowadays, and for good reason. Plenty of scientific research supports the fact that consistently practicing gratitude is good for you, both mentally and even physically. People who live by this core value sleep better, have less stress and anxiety, and are generally more resilient to the ups and downs of life.

But the truth is, **showing appreciation and gratitude is great for your business as well**. The benefits extend far past yourself and your own personal happiness.

That's why you want to make this part of your daily work life!

Think about it this way. Say you make a purchase from a company and receive a note of appreciation that is totally unexpected and heartfelt. Say you're in the middle of a really crappy day when you get this note. You are likely going to stop, even for a second, and get out of your own head. You're going to think something along the lines of, *Wow. That was so nice to receive. What a cool gesture.* Almost like a deep breath or a reset button.

You're going to associate those positive feelings with that company.

You're going to remember that this company went out of their way to make you feel that you were appreciated, that your purchase mattered. You're going to feel not like a member of a transaction but like a valued customer . . . because you are!

So the next time you need to make a similar purchase, or maybe buy a gift for a friend, you're going to want to support that business again.

My business specializes in making planners and high-quality paper products. Paper products aren't exactly in short supply. Planners are a dime a dozen on Amazon and in every Dollar Store in town.

So if there's no shortage of planners and paper out there, how can I make mine special? How can I make it so people trust my company and brand and want to come back, year after year? The answer for me is easy—through gratitude.

The great news I've found is that once you're in the habit of practicing gratitude and appreciation and start seeing just how much it benefits you, your teams, and your business as a whole, you'll be hooked. So whether it's been a few years since you've written a thank-you note or you can't remember the last time you thanked one of the vendors who make your life easier, this chapter is for you.

GRATITUDE WITH INTENTION

Let's just get this part out of the way, and make sure we're all super clear about something:

Fake gratitude is *not* gratitude.

Let me give you an example. Remember the story from chapter 1 about Brenda, the woman who came up to me at a speaking event and showered me with fake compliments in order to get me to "tell my friends" about her product? And how that was a perfect example of how *not* to build a relationship with someone?

It's similar with gratitude.

Remember, we're starting with a **relationships-first** mentality. People can smell a disingenuous person from a mile away. They can also smell disingenuous *appreciation* from a mile away.

FAKE GRATITUDE
is *not*
GRATITUDE.

This chapter is not about teaching you how to show gratitude in order to get what you want from someone (e.g., shower them with fake compliments or gifts). If you ask me, that's not gratitude. That's marketing. Bad marketing, at that.

I'm talking about *gratitude with intention*.

Here's what I mean. After a few hard lessons at my flower shop, I eventually got into a good groove and built a solid business. I was very aware that my business wasn't just run by me alone. I was dependent on my vendors, my team members, and my customers to keep it thriving. Without them, there would be no success.

I got into the habit of sitting down every Friday and thinking of someone to write a thank-you note to. A customer, a team member, the mail carrier, it didn't matter. *Someone in my life* was going to get a handwritten thank-you note from me.

There was no motivation for me beyond simply living my values. It felt good to me to write a thank-you note, and that was it. No ulterior motives or expectations.

Sometimes people would let me know how nice it was to receive my notes. Sometimes not. It didn't matter, because my intention wasn't to receive praise. The act of writing the note was enough for me.

Now that we have texting and social media, showing this sort of quick and meaningful type of gratitude is even easier. You don't need a pen or nice stationery anymore—a simple text or a quick email letting someone know you appreciate their help, idea, or purchase is great.* So send that note with no caveats or ulterior motives.

---

*   I will note here that handwritten notes are a great practice and seem to always mean a little more to someone. I always say "put your time on paper." With everyone so busy, living with such chaotic schedules, receiving a handwritten note isn't just about the note itself. It's about knowing the person who sent it took the time to sit and write it, address the envelope, stamp it, and drop it in a mailbox for pick-up. The time they spent doing that was for *you*, and could never be duplicated in an email or text message!

The nice thing is that this isn't rocket science. We'll talk in the next section about ideas for showing gratitude in business, but keep in mind that sometimes simple is best. **Don't overthink it. And above all, don't have any expectations around it.**

SHOWING GRATITUDE

This is going to sound cheesy, but hear me out. Probably the most obvious way I show gratitude is the old-fashioned way, through thank-you notes and little gifts—not just on holidays or birthdays, but as surprises, when people are least expecting them. One of the best things about building solid relationships with my teams, vendors, and customers is that I get to know them as people. When I see something they'll love or have the opportunity to surprise them with a note to make sure they know how much I appreciate them, I jump on it.

But I get it. Not everyone is comfortable with this. You might be all in regarding the importance of gratitude, but constantly being on the lookout for surprise gifts and out-of-the-blue gestures to show appreciation might feel a little too far outside your comfort zone.

If that's you, don't worry about it. Again, no need to overthink things. Here are some ways I see leaders and business owners get into a habit of showing gratitude that are beyond thank-you notes and don't require scouring the web for gift ideas:

- **A heartfelt social media post.** No matter what your business is, having someone post about your product and how it's impacted their life in a positive way feels great. When that happens for you, thank them! Publicly! I'm often amazed when I see business owners miss this simple opportunity to show appreciation for their customers.
- **Share gratitude on your platforms.** Whether on social media, on your website, or at your next speaking event, if you have an opportunity to show appreciation to a person or an organization, do it in a heartfelt way.

DON'T OVERTHINK IT.
And above all, DON'T HAVE ANY EXPECTATIONS AROUND IT.

- **Gift cards.** Nowadays it's so easy to send people gift cards. Usually, in just a couple of clicks of a mouse, you're done. Starbucks and Target are fine, but you also have the opportunity to patronize another small business you love and give a gift card to support them too. That's a win-win.
- **Celebrate completed projects.** At The Paper & Plan Co, we are constantly launching new products. I know how hard my team works to make sure each and every detail is covered so our customers are satisfied. We always celebrate in some little way, as a way of showing how much I appreciate them.
- **Keep a gratitude journal.** I know, I know. This is borderline woo-woo, but give it a chance. Remember in the last chapter when I told you about how powerful it can be to get all your issues and challenges down on paper so you can figure out how to solve them? Keeping a journal of all you have to be grateful for can serve a similar, mind-settling purpose. Try it and see what I mean. Get into the habit of somehow, some way, acknowledging your good fortune on a regular basis. Write it down so you can see it.

And I know what you're thinking: *I don't have to do this when I've had a super shitty day, right? Please say I don't have to do this when I've had a super shitty day...* Oh, yes. I want you to practice gratitude especially when you've had a shitty day. It will help you get back to work the next day with a clear head and (hopefully) a better attitude.

It is so easy to get started on this right now. Part of my morning routine is writing down three things I'm grateful for. I do this every single day. It's as much a part of my morning as brushing my teeth or taking a shower. It helps to start my day with a grateful heart and mindset. You can do this before bed, at lunch, whenever. Just make it part of your daily practice.

GRATITUDE EVEN WHEN IT'S **HARD**

It's easy to be grateful for the good things. Once you're in the habit of showing gratitude for all the ways things are going right, you'll see what I mean. Gratitude and happiness go hand in hand.

But what about the bad stuff?

Be grateful for *that* shit too.

Here's what I mean. For the longest time, I would allow someone's negative experience with my business to ruin my day. It could have been an unhappy customer, a negative review, a difficult conversation with a team member, or a miscommunication with a vendor. You name it—if it was negative, I would let it weigh on me like a ton of bricks.

As I've gotten older and wiser, I know that those negative experiences, while not fun, are opportunities for growth.

And as you know by now from this book, you should be seeking out opportunities for growth consistently. **Opportunities for growth are something to be grateful for.**

Success isn't about making everyone happy all the time. That's why I'm so conscious of running my business by the core values that I have created for myself. The hard truth is that you *can't* make everyone happy all the time. You *will* have hard conversations. People will let you down, and you will let them down.

Those difficult times don't mean you aren't succeeding as an entrepreneur and leader. In fact, they're a *gift* to you as an entrepreneur and leader.

- **Negative review?** Someone took the time out to write that review, and there might be something in there that you can really learn and improve from.

Opportunities for growth ARE SOMETHING TO BE **GRATEFUL FOR.**

- **Unhappy customer?** You have the opportunity to see things from their perspective and make the situation right.
- **Difficult situation with a vendor or a team member?** You can get heated, even disagree wholeheartedly, and still be thankful you have had the experience so you can do better next time.

We live in a time where so much of what we do is done publicly, and on social media. I see people get emotional, condescending, and even hateful as a result of something negative that has happened to them and their business. I get it. Sometimes it's really hard to separate the emotion from the situation.

But there's a danger in being quick to jump to conclusions and comebacks. This is true online, but also true in person. Keep in mind that if you can come from a place of gratitude—even for the hard times—you'll be much better equipped to come up with solutions.

Likewise, if someone comes at you with negativity and hate, you have the opportunity to disarm them with gratitude. You can come from a place of seeing the humanity in the other person and acknowledging their experience.

I'm sorry to hear about your bad experience. Here's how I can make it right.

I understand your frustration and am grateful you took the time to reach out.

I'm disappointed to hear you weren't pleased with my product, but I appreciate you trying it.

It's too bad we don't agree on this particular issue, but I'm still grateful for your support.

See what I mean? **Gratitude works to *strengthen* relationships, even when it's hard.** Even when the outcome isn't what you wanted.

Relationships first.

GRATITUDE WORKS TO *STRENGTHEN* RELATIONSHIPS, even when it's hard.

NOW MORE THAN EVER

As I write this book, we are dealing with massive labor shortages and supply chain issues as a result of the COVID-19 pandemic. My teams and I are working around the clock to make sure we have done all we can to provide the best products we possibly can, but the truth is that the holidays are around the corner, and the first of the year is always pretty important when you're in the business of making yearly planners. There's plenty I can control, but plenty I can't.

You are handling any number of issues around your business too. No matter where you are in your entrepreneurship path, you'll be dealing with hard things and making tough decisions.

People come to me for the truth, so here it is. **When you sign up for the life of the entrepreneur, you're signing up for all of it. The good, the bad, and the ugly.** It's easy to be grateful for the good stuff, but you have the choice to lead with gratitude and appreciation even when it's hard.

I'm not saying you need to be positive all the time. Toxic positivity and gratitude are two very different things. What I'm saying is that appreciating the life and experiences you've had, which have brought you to where you are in your business, is going to do wonders for your well-being.

This is true now more than ever.

Your teams deserve the best version of you, as do your vendors and your customers. *You* deserve the best version of you! Being grateful and appreciative of the journey—even the shitty parts—is where it begins.

9
HAVE FUN AND THINK BIG

WHEN I FIRST STARTED PUTTING TOGETHER this book, I assumed that this final chapter, "Have Fun and Think Big," would go first. It's my "first" core value, after all. So what happened?

As I started thinking about it, "Have Fun and Think Big" can sound like some of that cosmic backrub style woo-woo cheerleading BS we hear all the time from social influencers. Don't get me wrong—it's an important part of the entrepreneur's mindset, something I obviously value and want you to value too. But as much as you're starting your business from your passion and leading with that place of adding value and being open to new ideas and opportunities, I didn't want anyone to read that first chapter and think that the good ideas—the fun stuff—are the stuff you lead with.

You're leading with relationships, remember? **Relationships first.**

The good news is that this core value, along with all the core values that I've outlined in this book, isn't ranked by importance and doesn't belong in any certain order. You're going to be leading with your core values at all times.

Having fun and thinking big is going to be part of your philosophy from the moment your great idea comes to you, to every day you spend building your business. And that is a great thing!

LEADING WITH INSPIRATION

I don't need to define the concepts of "having fun" and "thinking big" for you. You know what those things mean! What I do think is important is making sure you know that having fun and thinking big should be tied directly to your core values.

In my case, having fun and thinking big ties directly to my mentality of **relationships first.** Thinking back to my flower-shop days, my inspiration for starting that business wasn't some sort of lightning strike from out of nowhere. It came directly from seeing a need in my community and knowing I could fill it. My small farm town needed a boutique, something high-end, something that would make event planning easier. I simply followed the inspiration as I built that business. I added tuxedo rentals, wedding planning, and beautiful in-home decorating services.

It was fun and easy for me to

THINK BIG

WHEN I FOCUSED ON THE NEEDS OF MY CUSTOMERS.

It was fun and easy for me to think big when I focused on the needs of my customers.

The same thing happened when I started writing cookbooks. I was getting serious about my health and found myself shopping for cookbooks that simply didn't work for me. I didn't have time for long, complicated recipes with a million ingredients. I knew I could help other busy people like myself, and I followed that inspiration.

And the same thing happened *again* when I started The Paper & Plan Co. The idea for creating a planner company didn't come from nowhere. It sprang directly from seeing a need for a specific type and quality of planner, and grew from there.

You'll see that following your inspiration isn't just reserved for your business itself. My inspiration has led me to start my Women in Business Workshop too. After sixteen years as an entrepreneur, I found myself totally over all the fake froufrou stuff I was seeing all over the place. I obviously wanted to connect with other driven entrepreneurs, but I wanted to do so in an environment I was comfortable in, with women who were ready to dominate in their field. Women who realized that glitter doesn't pay the bills, hard work does.

This isn't to say I got ideas and then dove headfirst into the deep end. There are strategies and game plans that need to be put into place, and we'll talk more about that later in the chapter. It's not uncommon for an entrepreneur to get so excited by their big, badass idea that they launch too early or don't take the time to build their platforms, presence, and most importantly, relationships.

You've come far enough along in this book to know that not everything about building a business is "fun." There will be hard days, weeks, months, and even years. For me, I wouldn't classify the day-to-day operations of running a business as "fun." That's why I'm so focused on gratitude and seeking inspiration as a daily practice. It's how I incorporate fun into every day.

Any entrepreneur will tell you that there is fun in overcoming challenges. From the day-to-day logistics to the big old shitstorms that threaten to derail you, the secret to your success probably doesn't lie in a bolt of lightning from the sky. It's probably more connected to your ability to have fun while weathering the storms. It's about finding the fun to get you through, because the further you get in your entrepreneur's journey, the hardest times are the best memories to look back on.

LITTLE WINS

I wish I could tell you I have some sort of cool, fun hobby that keeps me occupied during my "down time," but the truth is I'm boring and like to create a life with minimal down time. I don't really have hobbies apart from a love of organizing and obsessing over my English bulldogs. If you have a great, fun hobby, I encourage you to keep it! Incorporating fun into your life is important.

For me, work is fun. I'm not just saying that. It really, truly is. I thrive on the challenge of building and maintaining my businesses and growing the other companies and brands I'm involved in. I've built these amazing teams around me, all focused on the same big vision, and this pushes me to work even harder. As I reflect, I think it's because I've always been an athlete. I see work and business as a game, one I'm constantly competing in. **Every day is practice, and every day is game day.**

This isn't to say that you are always competing against other teams, necessarily. Sure, there is competition out there, but there's more to being an athlete than your performance on game day. Athletes are constantly improving themselves, preparing, and learning. I think of these day-to-day improvements as sharpening my competitive spear.

In my experience, all great leaders have this competitive spirit within them. Without it, when the going gets tough, you run the risk of raising the white flag and deciding that it's just too hard to continue.

I get it. And that's precisely why I want each of you to think of all the business building as *fun*. Each and every day, even with the things that are challenging. **I want you to see each challenge and situation as an opportunity for you to grow and learn**.

Of course, we all want the "big win," whatever that means for you. But until then, celebrate the little wins! Celebrate when your first order comes

EVERY DAY IS PRACTICE, and every day is GAME DAY.

through, when you get your first positive review, when you meet your next deadline. Allow yourself to enjoy it! Don't wait to have fun until you have some sort of big payday. Let every little win count. However, don't get stuck in this celebration mode. Do a little happy dance or whatever sets your sail, then get back to work. Just like in sports—if you score a goal, you take a minute to celebrate with your team. Then it's back to the huddle to craft the next play to win. And **even after the victory, it's not about winning the game that day—it's about winning the championship year after year. It's about legacy building.**

THINKING BIG

I've said it before in this book, but it's worth repeating in this final chapter: you are never going to reach your full potential. Your "full potential" is a sliding scale, a journey without an end. This means that instead of working toward a final goal for yourself, you're focused on always growing and reaching bigger and higher.

As a business owner, this will mean a couple of things:
- "Thinking big" is a part of everyday life, from the beginning to the middle all the way to the end of your business. Think so big that it scares you . . . terrifies you.
- The harder you make your goals to reach, the harder you'll try. Celebrate the small wins while aggressively working toward huge goals.

When I talk about thinking big, I don't necessarily mean you should be working toward a monetary goal, though that is one thing. I want you to think even bigger than finances or reaching toward a specific emotion or feeling. I want you to feel excited just by the *prospect* of thinking big and setting new goals.

You already know that I keep a detailed planner for myself with my daily tasks and goals, but thinking big for me also means setting huge yearly goals at the beginning of each year. That way, when I'm setting my daily goals,

I have my bigger goals in mind. My tasks have a bigger meaning beyond just getting me through the day—they're seeing me to my next stage of growth, and the next stage of growth after that.

You might find this to be counterintuitive to the last chapter on gratitude. Didn't I just tell you that one of my core values was to stay grounded in gratitude at all times, and to be grateful for failures and challenges? Yes! But the way I see it, **there's a fine line between staying complacent in a bubble of gratitude and pushing yourself beyond your comfort zone.**

I figure that the more I can do as an entrepreneur, the more I can make an impact on people's lives. It's as simple as that. So yes, every night for the last sixteen years, when I say my prayers, I say, "Thank you for what I've been given. If I wake up tomorrow with nothing more than I was given today, I'd be grateful." But I also see it as my obligation to focus on not just my own happiness, but the happiness of others as well.

It will be like that for you too. Whether or not you believe in a higher power or purpose, finding that balance between being grateful for what you have and pushing yourself for more is absolutely key.

A RISK YOU'RE WILLING TO TAKE

I've been able to see firsthand the power of thinking big through my husband, Andy. When we first started dating, his company, 1st Phorm International, was just five months old. At the time, we used our garage to store products. I vividly remember having ten boxes of protein powder in the garage at one point. When we would arrive home, we would park outside the garage, walk up to the keypad, and quickly put in the code. Then, as soon as the garage door was up just enough, we would duck under it to get inside, then close it as fast as possible so the neighbors wouldn't know that we were storing products in our garage.

There's a fine line between STAYING COMPLACENT IN A BUBBLE OF GRATITUDE AND PUSHING YOURSELF BEYOND YOUR COMFORT ZONE.

At one point in those early days, I remember driving on the interstate with Andy. He pointed to a large plot of land just off the interstate and matter-of-factly said, "That's where 1st Phorm will be one day." He saw the entire thing clearly and shared his vision with me: a state-of-the-art facility that would rival any corporation. He saw it as a place for professional athletes to come and train, a place where people would want to travel just to get a tour, a facility that would give back in big ways to the community, employing hundreds and hundreds of people inside its four walls and offering careers to thousands outside those walls. He had the vision for what the company would become—and the company would eventually exceed those expectations.

Did it take time? Of course it did. It took ten years and a lot of hard work, discipline, and dedication to make that dream come true, but it did. All because he was vigilant about not losing sight of the big picture. His excitement and dedication were inspirational to me as I built my businesses.

There are so many other stories of entrepreneurs who owe their success to constantly finding inspiration and thinking big. One memory that always stands out to me is the time I met Steve Wozniak, one of the founders of Apple. We'd invited him to speak at an entrepreneurship summit about leadership, and to be honest, I was not prepared for what I saw. I suppose I'd been expecting a serious, Silicon Valley tech guy, but Woz was nothing like that.

When he spoke about his past, his successes and failures, and his vision for the future, he was downright giddy. I kept thinking he seemed like a little boy, excited to tell the whole world about his latest invention. His work was clearly fun for him, and he had a childlike wonder about all his passion projects. His excitement was infectious.

That's what I want for you. **I want you to take your core values, look at the work you have to do to build and improve your business, and see it as a fun and exciting challenge.**

WHEN YOU ARE **LEADING WITH** YOUR PASSIONS *it's hard to go wrong.*

And if you think to yourself that this level of forward thinking and creative excitement isn't for you, that's okay! Plenty of people aren't cut out for the high-level risks associated with starting your own business. Social media nowadays makes everyone think that they need to be an entrepreneur, but nothing could be further from the truth. You don't have to start your own business from the ground up; you can be a successful IN-trepreneur and innovate within another company.

When you are leading with your passions, it's hard to go wrong. The way I see it, investment (which some call a sacrifice, but truly is an investment in your future) is part of the deal. If you choose to take the risk of starting a business, make it a risk you're *willing* to take.

READY TO ROLL

How will you know when to act on your next big, badass idea? For me, the answer to this is pretty simple. It's about solving problems. When you've seen a need and figured out a way to address that need, you'll come to a crossroads. You'll have the choice between moving forward down the path of starting your own business or not.

I know it's time to move forward when I can't stop thinking about it. When my love of the idea is all-consuming. When I know that I can have fun and think big continuously as a result of growing this idea and seeing where it takes me.

This book has laid out the core values that I've put in place to create a culture and businesses with a winning spirit.

I don't know everything. I am a constant student of learning what works best. I've had my ups and downs, but I wouldn't have it any other way. You'll have your own core values, and you'll have your own ups and downs. To me, that's the fun of it—that's the adventure of entrepreneurship. It will be the fun of it for you too.

So as you work within your company or build your business, I want to leave you with a few last pieces of advice to see you through.

- Establish a solid social media presence. This will take years to build and a lot of effort, but it's so worth it. Work on driving traffic to your website and email list. Create buzz!
- Establish your brand. Make it something you can stick behind and be proud of.
- Identify your ideal customer and target audience.
- Create a great product.
- Set your goals, your core values, and your mission. Look at them daily as a reminder of what you're working toward.

In other words, **relationships first**. Build them, maintain them. Show people who you are and what you stand for. No frills. No BS. Create trust and a solid foundation.

And then buckle up for a long, sometimes bumpy, but ultimately awesome ride while creating your legacy.

1. RELATIONSHIPS **FIRST**
2. **MAKE** IT YOUR BEST WORK
3. PERSONAL **ACCOUNTABILITY**
4. **RESPECT** THE POTENTIAL AND SIGNIFICANCE OF **EVERY PERSON**
5. NEVER COMPROMISE **TRUTH**
6. ACT WITH HONESTY AND **INTEGRITY**
7. **PROMOTE** A CULTURE OF INNOVATION AND CONTINUOUS **IMPROVEMENT**
8. SHOW APPRECIATION AND **GRATITUDE**
9. HAVE FUN AND **THINK BIG**

QUESTIONS
FOR FURTHER DISCUSSION

CHAPTER 1: RELATIONSHIPS FIRST

What have I done this week to cultivate new relationships?

What do I have to offer others in a relationship without expecting anything in return?

Am I being intentional with building relationships?

How do I show appreciation for the relationships I have built both professionally and personally?

What are some ways I can improve my relationship-building skills?

1.

2.

3.

4.

5.

CHAPTER 2: MAKE IT YOUR BEST WORK

What does my product/offering reflect about my personal standard?

Would I be thrilled to receive my product or offering as a customer?

Three ways I can improve my product:
1.

2.

3.

Do I operate consistently in a "make it my best work" mentality?

Is how I lead my team, family, and community my best work?
If not, how can I improve?

CHAPTER 3: PERSONAL ACCOUNTABILITY

How do I define personal accountability?

Do I have anyone on my team that is a momentum taker or breaker?

What do I do to hold my team accountable and instill the practice of holding themselves accountable?

Have I been setting my Top Five Priorities every day to hold myself accountable? Do I encourage this in my team as well?

My top three short-term goals I need to plan backward for and hold myself accountable to are:

1.

2.

3.

CHAPTER 4: RESPECT THE POTENTIAL AND SIGNIFICANCE OF EVERY PERSON

Am I encouraging a growth mindset within my organization?

Does my team feel encouraged to step up into leadership roles and even create new roles?

Do I actively seek the potential of everyone on my team and also in my personal life?

Am I hiring based on what someone can do or more for who they are as a person?

What are three things I can change to improve my interview process?
1.

2.

3.

CHAPTER 5: NEVER COMPROMISE TRUTH

How do I define Never Compromise Truth?

Do I often hit the panic button before I hit the process button?

Do I lead and live by my core values while also keeping the humanity of the people I'm surrounded by intact?

Am I offering direct, clear, and kind communication to my team, customers, and vendors? What are three ways I can improve on this?

1.

2.

3.

As I reflect on lessons I have learned as a leader/entrepreneur that would help young leaders, what would the overarching message be?

CHAPTER 6: ACT WITH HONESTY AND INTEGRITY

Who in my life exhibits integrity at all times?

When have my integrity and honesty been tested most recently? How did I handle it?

How would someone currently rate my customer service on a scale from 1–5, with 1 being the worst and 5 being the best?

Do I provide customer service or customer care?

What are three ways I can improve my customer experience?

1.

2.

3.

CHAPTER 7: PROMOTE A CULTURE OF INNOVATION AND CONTINUOUS IMPROVEMENT

What does innovation mean to me?

How am I disrupting my industry?

Of the four types of innovation, which type fits my business best at the current moment?

Three ways I can work to create a culture of innovation and improvement are:
1.

2.

3.

CHAPTER 8: SHOW APPRECIATION AND GRATITUDE

Do I practice gratitude daily?

Do I show appreciation to others? How can I make it more impactful?

How am I exercising gratitude in a negative situation?

What am I grateful for in this moment?
1.

2.

3.

CHAPTER 9: HAVE FUN AND THINK BIG

What are my personal/professional core values?

Where or how do I find inspiration?

What is my big vision for my future?

An idea that I cannot quit thinking about is . . .

What are five ways I'm showing up on social media to build my brand?
1.

2.

3.

4.

5.

ABOUT THE AUTHOR

Emily Frisella is a multi-passionate entrepreneur who started her first brick-and-mortar business at the age of twenty. She is the founder of The Paper & Plan Co. and the author of the Amazon best-selling cookbooks *The Fresh Farmhouse Kitchen* and *The Saint's Plate & The Sinner's Dinner*. Emily is the founder of The Women in Business Workshop, COO of 44Seven Media, COO of Arete Syndicate, cohost of *Curious Me* podcast, cofounder of the Freedom Reads book club, business coach, and speaker.

Emily encourages entrepreneurs to use their voice and reach their potential in their personal and professional lives through self-development, accountability, awareness, and building authentic relationships. She is based in St. Louis, Missouri.

To find out more about Emily Frisella, visit **EmilyFrisella.com**.